Ernest Ingersoll

Wild Neighors

Out-Door Studies in the United States

Ernest Ingersoll

Wild Neighors
Out-Door Studies in the United States

ISBN/EAN: 9783337186012

Printed in Europe, USA, Canada, Australia, Japan

Cover: Foto ©ninafisch / pixelio.de

More available books at **www.hansebooks.com**

WILD NEIGHBORS

To Her

My Wife

ACKNOWLEDGMENT

THE substance of several of the essays, or of parts of them, that follow, has been printed heretofore in *The Field* (of London), *Harper's Magazine*, *The Popular Science Monthly*, *The Evening Post* (of New York), or *Frank Leslie's Popular Monthly*. The author desires to credit these publications with this priority, and to thank them for permitting him to make this new and revised use of the material.

CONTENTS

ix

LIST OF ILLUSTRATIONS

xi

WILD NEIGHBORS

I

OUR GRAY SQUIRRELS

Down past my window, as I sit writing beside it, falls a twig from the black oak at the corner of the house. Half a minute later another sinks wavering downward, buoyed by its broad leaves, which are green and healthy. This happens in July, far in advance of their natural time to fall. What is the cause? A glance informs me. One of our gray squirrels is out on the end of an overhanging limb, and I am just in time to see him bite off another leafy twig and carry it away. It is evident that he had dropped the other one accidentally. What is he doing? I vault out of the window, and keep him in view as he makes his way nearly to the summit of a tall white oak, where he leaves his branch as a contribution to a half bushel or so of sticks and leaves lodged in a convenient notch. Another squirrel is there, and together they scramble over the mass, packing and entangling it together, and occasionally disappear-

B   I

ing into its interior, showing that it is hollow. There seems, however, to be no special entrance, the inmates pushing their way into the centre, and escaping from it wherever it seems easiest to part the twigs. I have never seen more than one pair at work upon any one nest. The work is done mainly in the early morning, and the task is accomplished very speedily.

I know this particular pair of squirrels very well. They have been tenants of the grove ever since we came to live in this edge of the city, and though the town has now grown beyond and around us, and the grove is given a perpetual moonlight from the electric lamp on the corner, the trees and bushes remain. In midsummer they may indulge their fondness for toadstools, upon which, during August, they seem almost wholly to subsist. Nuts and acorns come with each returning autumn, and in midwinter provender is spread upon friendly window-sills.

Almost the only advantage the squirrels have taken of civilization, however, has been to occupy the boxes that my benevolent neighbor, Dr. J. P. Phillips, has put up for them in the trees, which are tenanted more or less all the year round, one family occupying each box and tree by itself as long as it wishes, and putting in its own furniture — a new bedroom set of grass and soft leaves. Of these boxes they distinctly prefer those which are simply sections of hollow logs, probably because nearest like the natural cavities in decayed tree-trunks chosen (in cold latitudes) by the squirrels as their home; but as none of our pets had been forest bred, this preference seems to have been dictated by an inherited taste. By midsummer these tenements become so hot and vermin-infested that the squirrels leave them and construct bowers of leaves, as my friends in the oak were doing when they attracted my attention; and they occasionally inhabit them all winter, when the family nestles into the fluffy mass of loose leaves and grass forming the centre of the ball, and thus keeps warm.

Though their nests and burrows become more or less infected with vermin, all our squirrels are exceedingly cleanly animals, and spend much time in rubbing their faces and cleansing their own fur and that of their young ones. "When they accidentally step into the water," writes Godman, "they make use of their bushy tail for the purpose of drying themselves, passing it several times through their hands."

This squirrel is the one which in the older books is called the Northern gray squirrel, *Sciurus migratorius*, in contrast with the Southern gray squirrel. Several other closely related species have been described from the interior and the Pacific coast, besides the very distinct "fox," "red," "flying," and other sharply distinguished members of the family. Certain differences of size and coat notice-

able between types of our gray squirrel from widely
separated regions, accompanied by local peculiarities of habit, at first misled naturalists, but only one
species is now recognized, — *Sciurus carolinensis.*

The first litter of young among the wild gray
squirrels is seen in March in the warmer parts of
the country, and somewhat later in the more northern States and in Canada. At least one more
brood usually follows before winter. Our friends
in the grove, however, sure of food and lodging,
bring out their broods with little regard to season.
One female, which has been known to us for years
as the "mother squirrel," seems rarely without a
family; and Dr. Phillips assures me that he has
known her to bear four litters in a single twelve-
month, thus braving all sorts of weather.

This exhibits the hardihood of these little animals. No weather seems cold enough to daunt
them. They endure the semi-arctic climate north
of Lake Superior, remain all the year on the peaks
of the Adirondacks, where their only food is the
seeds of the black spruce, and appear in midwinter
in Manitoba; but when a sleet storm comes, and
every branch and twig is encased in ice, then the
squirrel stays at home. I remember one such storm
which was of unusual severity and did vast damage.
The ice clothed the trees for several days in succession, and the imprisoned animals became very
hungry. The Doctor and I had swung from tree
to tree a line of bridges made of poles along which

the squirrels scampered, no less to their delight than to ours, often leaping one over the other with extraordinary agility and grace when two met on this single-track, air-line road.

One of these bridges led to a window-sill in each residence, where food was often spread, and it was amusing to see the circumspection with which, at last, they crept toward it along the icy poles, digging their claws into the glazed surface, and often slipping astride or almost off the bridge.

In the tree-tops, where they rush and leap at full speed, they are by no means safe from falling, but usually manage to catch hold somewhere, often by only a single toe, apparently, yet are able to lift the body up, like gymnasts, to a firmer foothold. Their strength is remarkable, especially in the region of the great hams, whose development accounts for the really astonishing leaping powers these animals possess.

Should they fall clear to the ground, as sometimes happens, they alight right side up like a cat, and seem none the worse for the accident. The feet are wide-spread in such a case, and the loose skin over the ribs is stretched and flattened out very perceptibly. It would seem only a step from that condition to the parachute with which the flying-squirrel is provided; but if the development of this formation in the latter came about through natural selection, it must have begun very long ago, for Cope has found a fossil (*Allomys*), which he considers representative of the flying-squirrel type, as far back as the Jurassic. I have read of a Mexican squirrel that was thrown from a cliff several hundred feet high, as an experiment, which spread its body and settled easily to a safe alighting upon the ground.

Dr. C. C. Abbott notes that a certain sycamore near his home on the Delaware was avoided by the squirrels, and accounts for it by the supposition that its scaly bark caused them too many falls; but they are incessantly climbing the shagbark hickories, — far worse than the buttonball in the matter of roughness. The latter tree, however, rewards them in nuts, while the sycamore had nothing to give them, and the truth probably is that Abbott's squirrels were wise enough not to inconvenience themselves for nothing.

The spring and early summer is most uniformly the season of reproduction, and this is the period when we see least of our pets. The mothers are awaiting the birth of their annual, or perhaps semi-annual broods, and spend most of their time at rest in their homes, while all the males of the grove go wandering away to visit other temporary bachelors. To call them all *temporary husbands*, would be nearer truth, however, for, so far as we can discover, the mating is only for a single season, and as soon as gestation begins, the mothers become vixenish, and not only turn their husbands out-of-doors, but expel them from the premises.

Usually four kittens arrive in one litter, blind
and helpless, and during the first month remain
within the nest, closely attended by the mother,
who permits no other squirrel — even her pre-
sumed mate — to come near her. Each family,
in fact, pre-empts a tree, and their sense of property is so strong that usually a trespasser will
depart with little resistance, as if conscious of
being where he has no right. Old males will
sometimes kill their young, so that the mother
does well to keep all at a distance.

At the end of a month the young are half grown,
and begin to scramble awkwardly about their doorway, yet the mother won't let them leave the nest
until she thinks they are fully ready.

One morning in the middle of October I observed that a family of four young squirrels was
venturing forth from a box just outside my study
window. They were not more than six weeks old,
and were very timid. It was not often that more
than two or three would appear at once, and one
of these seemed much farther advanced than the
rest, while another was very babyish. Their prime
characteristic was inquisitiveness. What a fine and
curious new world was this they had been introduced
to! How much there was to see! How many delightful things to do! They ceaselessly investigated
everything about them with minute attention, and
had very pretty ways, such as a habit of clasping
each other in their arms around the neck. They

frequently scratched and stroked one another, and once I saw one diligently combing another's tail with its fore feet.

The tail, indeed, which is flat, and has the wavy hair growing laterally from a careful parting along the muscular midrib, is an object of great pride to its owner. It is, no doubt, useful and comforting as a wrapper in cold weather, and certainly assists the agile acrobat as a balancing-pole; but that it is highly appreciated purely as an ornament, is very evident from the abashed demeanor of the little animal when a portion of its brush is lost.

The generic name *Sciurus* (from which comes "squirrel," through Old French *esquirel*) is derived from Greek words meaning a creature which sits under the shadow of its tail, and the name shade-tail is in actual use in some of the Southern States to-day. We might appropriately translate the Greek in this case as designating an animal whose tail puts all the rest of him into the shade.

Gradually they gain strength and confidence, and then you will see how far the liveliness of the young can surpass even the tireless activity of old squirrels. Both old and young are exceedingly fond of play, springing from the ground as if in a high-jumping match, and turning regular summer-saults in the grass; but the most amusing thing is this: Finding a place where the tip of a tough branch hangs almost to the ground, they will leap up and catch it, sometimes with only one hand,

and then swing back and forth with the greatest glee, just like boys who discover a grape-vine in the woods or a dangling rope in a gymnasium. These and many similar antics seem to be done "just for fun."

The kittens continue to be nursed by the mother until they have grown to be almost as heavy as herself. It seems impossible that her system can stand such a drain, — in fact she does grow weak and thin, — and my neighbor, who has been an extremely close observer of their economy for several years, has come to the conclusion that the mother weans the kittens gradually by giving them food which she has regurgitated, or, at any rate, has thoroughly chewed up in her own mouth.

No animal is more motherly than one of these parent squirrels, and it is delightful to watch her behavior when the nearly grown brood has begun to make short excursions, and is undergoing instruction. All the other families in the grove take an interest in the proceedings, and chatter about it at a great rate; but if one comes too near and attempts any interference in the instruction, he is likely to be driven away most vigorously by the jealous mother. Every morning lessons in climbing and nut-hunting are given, and pretty scenes are enacted. The pride of the little mother as she leads her train out on some aerial path is very noticeable. They are slow and timid about following. Squirrels must learn to balance themselves on the pliant limbs by slow degrees. It is many a long day after they are able to chase one another up and down and under and around a rough oak trunk, in the liveliest game of tag ever witnessed, before they can skip about the branches and leap from one to the other with confidence in their security. The patient mother understands this, and encourages them very gently to "try, try again." I remember one such lesson. The old one marched ahead slowly, uttering low notes, as if to say : "Come on, my dears. Don't be afraid!" Every little while she would stop, and the two well-grown children following would creep up to her, and put their arms around her neck in the most human fashion, as if protesting that it was almost too hard a task.

This loving-kindness is extended to other young squirrels whenever no question of family rivalry interferes, as is shown, in a most amiable way, by incidents I have narrated elsewhere.

In spite of this I do not believe that, broadly speaking, the gray squirrel is a very intelligent animal, or has much brain-power. On the contrary, to my mind this squirrel, except within a very limited field, where a part of his brain has been developed by his necessities, is an unusually stupid animal. Dr. T. Wesley Mills of Montreal, who has made a study of brute psychology, has essayed to show that squirrels are the most intelligent of rodents; but even granting this (which I doubt, when I think of the rat), little is proved, and even Dr. Mills places the general intelligence of the red, the flying, and the ground squirrels superior to that of our gray, which he concedes to be deficient in docility.

Nevertheless, these animals within a certain narrow range of acts and motions are certainly sagacious; and they are somewhat teachable. It took our squirrels a very short time to learn that cracked nuts of several varieties, grains of corn, and other edibles were to be had on the window-sills. The squirrels know, furthermore, that the nuts are placed there from the inside, and if, as occasionally happens, the sill is empty, they will often stand up and tap upon the glass, as if to attract notice to their hunger.

Moreover, they know very well when the family meal-hours come around, and will present themselves at the windows pretty regularly then, since they have learned to expect more than ordinary attention at that time; and they do so even when, occasionally, the meal is omitted, so that no noise or odors of preparation could have apprised them of the time. The Doctor has had a few advance timorously to take food from his fingers, as the tame squirrels on Capitol Hill in Richmond, and in some other city parks, will do from almost any one.

It is plain that they recognize all of us as acquaintances from their indifference to our presence,

while they will raise a great clamor whenever a
stranger walks about under the trees.   More than
this, they seem to know the Doctor's horse and
carriage, and pay no attention to its goings and
comings, but become excited whenever another
vehicle enters the premises.   They will stay quietly
eating on the window-sill while one of us sits just
inside the glass, but when they see a visitor in the
room will almost invariably seize a nut and scamper
away as fast as they can go.   Furthermore their
actions convince us that when, as often happens
in midsummer, Dr. Phillips meets one of our squirrels in some far-away street, the little animal
recognizes him and shows its confidence in his
accustomed kindness; but I have never been
recognized in that way, to my knowledge.

As pets these squirrels are not greatly in demand, — not so much so as the flying-squirrels,
which crawl inside your coat and appeal to your
affection at once.   The grays are so mischievous,
trying their strong teeth on everything and dam-
aging furniture and hangings so rapidly, that we
never dared admit them to the house on terms of
intimacy, and as for confining them in a cage, it
was never thought of.

In spite of some stories I have heard and read,
I am under the impression that an attempt to
make a real pet of one would prove tiresome, if it
didn't fail altogether.   The animal is pretty to
look at, and pleasant to handle, but seems to have

little affection, or, at any rate, makes little demon-
stration of it.   It is selfish.   It wants you as a
friend only for what it can get out of you, and
these are not terms upon which love grows.   Its
big eyes are like jewels, but they never melt with
the fond delight of the dog in your companionship
and approval.   The squirrel may climb to your
shoulder, and explore your pockets for sweets;
but never will he leap into your lap and curl up
there for the enjoyment of being with you, and
purr contentedly over it as does your cat.   He has
no monkey-like antics with which to amuse you —
no melodious tones to beguile your ear; and one
who knows him as an acrobat of the tree-tops can
only look with pity upon his performance within
the limits of a whirling treadmill, such as is usually attached to squirrel cages.

Though the squirrels in this *rus in urbe* of our
grove have few enemies, they have never lost their
wariness.   Sometimes a tremendous clamor will
break out in the tree-tops — a mixture of sharp
ch-r-r-r-rs and whines, easily intelligible to us as
notes of alarm and indignation.   These usually
mean that a strange dog or cat is somewhere near.
No hawks or owls (save the little screech-owl) ever
come to disturb them, and, of course, none of the
wild-cats, weasels, or large serpents which kill
them in the wild forest is here to molest or make
them afraid, yet the population of the grove never
seems to increase, though the eight or ten pairs

more than double their numbers every six months.

The explanation is that the young leave us on coming to maturity. As a rule, their family had moved from the house where they were born to new quarters as soon as the young could take care of themselves, and here a new litter would soon be forthcoming.

These family flittings are often amusing spectacles. Sometimes the mother transports her kittens when blind and hairless, carrying them in her teeth; but generally she waits until they are able to travel. I recall one instance where early in the morning a mother had got her kittens down from the old nest to the end of a bridge that ran across to the chinquapin, in which her new home was to be. But to go out on that bridge was too much for the youngsters. She would run ahead, and one or two of them would creep after her a few yards, then suddenly become panic-stricken and scramble back. Again and again did the little mother, with endless patience and pains, counsel and entice them, until at last one was induced to keep a stout heart until he was safely over. Then ensued another interval of chattering and repeated trials and failures, and so the second and third were finally got across. It was now noon, and the poor squirrel looked quite fagged out, her ears drooped, her fur was ruffled, her movements had lost their *verve*, her tail hung low, and her cries became sharp and short. Her patience was exhausted. Instead of tenderly coaxing the last one of the four, she scolded at him, driving rather than leading the terrorized youngster along the shaky cable, and when it had reached the further tree, she seized it in her mouth, and fairly shoved it through the door of the new box.

It is probable that in their wild state, before their forest range was restricted and men began to slaughter them, all the arboreal squirrels were able by longevity and rapid increase to more than keep pace with the deaths in their ranks. Their natural term of life probably approaches twenty years. We have known continuously for twelve years one female who was apparently an old mother when she came, and is yet hale and hearty. During this time she has regularly produced at least two broods a year. At such a rate squirrels would multiply until they overbalanced the ratio of numbers assigned them by nature. Accounts by early writers show that they must formerly have been amazingly numerous. Godman says that the gray-coat was a fearful scourge to colonial farmers, and that Pennsylvania paid £8000 in bounties for their scalps during 1749 alone. This meant the destruction of 640,000 within a comparatively small district. In the early days of Western settlement regular hunts were organized by the inhabitants, who would range the woods in two companies from morning till night, vying as to which band should bring home the greater number of trophies; the quantities thus killed are almost incredible now.

Out of these excessive multitudes grew those sudden and seemingly aimless migrations of innumerable hosts of squirrels which justly excited wonder half a century ago. Thousands upon thousands, of this species usually, would suddenly appear in a locality, moving steadily in one direction. These migrations occurred only in warm weather, and at intervals of about five years, and all that I have been able to find notes upon were headed eastward. Nothing stopped the column, which would press forward through forests, prairies, and farm fields, over mountains and across broad rivers, such even as the Niagara, Hudson, and Mississippi. This little creature hates the water and is a bad swimmer, paddling clumsily along with his whole body and tail submerged. A large part, therefore, would be drowned, and those which managed to reach the opposite shore were so weary that many could be caught by the hand. Of course every floating object would be seized upon by the desperate swimmers, and thus arose the pretty fable that the squirrels ferried themselves over by launching and embarking upon chips, raising their tails as sails for their tiny rafts.

The motive which impelled the little migrants to gather in great companies from a wide area, and then in a vast coherent army to begin a movement, and continue it steadily in one direction for hundreds of miles, is hard to discover. It did not seem to be lack of food, for they were always fat. The migration was leisurely performed, too — never in too great a hurry to prevent feasting upon any fields of corn or sometimes of unripe grain that came in the way. Such a visitation, therefore, was like a flight of devouring locusts, one chronicler alleging that the sound they made in the maize in stripping off the husks to get at the succulent kernels was equal to that of a field full of men at harvesting. There is no difficulty, moreover, in judging of the effect such migrations. would have in restoring equilibrium in sciurine population, since, of the surplus which started, few survived long, and the remnant at last faded away among the Alleghanies or in some other distant locality without seeming to increase the number of squirrels there.

The curiosity and gayety of the gray squirrel are perhaps his strongest personal characteristics. Nothing unusual escapes his attention, and he is never satisfied until he knows all about it. He is the Paul Pry, the news-gatherer, of the woods.

When a new building is in course of erection in or near the grove, the workmen no sooner leave it than half a dozen squirrels go over and under and through it, examining every part. If I trim away branches and lay them in a heap, or repair a fence, or do anything else, Mr. Gray inspects it

c

thoroughly the moment my back is turned; and
when once the house was reoccupied after a long
vacancy, we caught the squirrels peeping in at the
windows and hopping gingerly to the sill of each
open door, to make sure the matter was all right.

It is most amusing to watch them on these tours
of inspection. Two or three times a day each one
makes the rounds of the premises, racing along
the fences, and into one tree after another, as if
to make certain that nothing had gone wrong.
He will halt on the summit of each post, rear up,
and look all about him; or, if his keen ears hear
an unwonted sound, will drop down upon all-fours,
ready to run, his tail held over his back like a
silver-edged plume, twitching nervously and jerk-
ing with each sharp utterance, as though it were
connected with his vocal organs by a string. "All
his movements," said Thoreau, "imply a spectator."

The excessive inquisitiveness I have described
often gets them into trouble, and is taken advantage of by their enemies. A wise serpent will coil
himself at the foot of a tree where squirrels are
playing, and will slowly wave his tail or display
his red tongue, sure that the squirrels will see him.
Doubtless they know him for what he is — a deadly
enemy; but they cannot resist a nearer look at
the curious object and that extraordinary motion.
Whining, chr-r-r-ring, barking, they creep down
the tree-trunk. The snake lies ready, his unwink-
ing eyes fixed upon the excited little quadruped.

Step by step, impelled by a fatal desire to learn more about that fascinating thing in the grass, Bunny steals forward — and is lost!

The male squirrels come back from their summer vagabondage looking very much the worse for wear, the result of many a battle, no doubt, for they are incorrigible fighters. In the season of courtship the males are especially pugnacious, and will bite one another severely, or hurl one another from lofty limbs.[1] The red squirrels, or chickarees, though hardly half as big, will whip the grays in a running fight every time; but when it comes to a clinch, the superior size and weight of the gray give him the victory. There is an eternal feud between them because the gray squirrels are continually raiding the hoards of nuts and acorns which the provident chickarees stow away in odd corners against the coming of winter. The holes in our long post-and-rail fence is a favorite place of deposition, and in autumn this fence is pretty regularly patrolled by a chickaree. If a reconnoitring gray even approaches this fence, the red will dash at him like wildfire.

One day a pan of shelled corn stood outside the

---

[1] There is no truth in the long-lived supposition that the victor in one of these knightly combats will emasculate his conquered foe. The only explanation, apart from an anatomical one, seems to be that the testicles of many squirrels are destroyed by a parasitic worm that is peculiar to those organs in the sciuri. They are also much troubled by subcutaneous parasites, particularly larvæ of flesh-flies of the genus Œstrus.

door of the Doctor's barn, and a chipmunk (the striped ground-squirrel) approached it cautiously from one side while a rat came from the barn on the other.   They met at the corn, whereupon, without an instant's hesitation, the chipmunk sprang into the air like a cat, and alighted squarely on the back of the rat, which, astounded and cowed by this unlooked-for attack, turned tail, shook off his fierce little foe, and raced for shelter, leaving chippie to fill his cheek-pouches at leisure and go home in triumph.

The only bird-enemy is the blue-jay, who seems to love to tease the squirrels in winter, just for mischief; and two jays, working together, can make it very unpleasant for Bunny.   One will dash at him with a joyous shout, whereupon the scared and nimble animal will slip around to the further side of the tree-trunk, "talking back" the while in the angriest language he knows; but there the other jay is ready for him, and he must immediately dodge back again to where the first is waiting to dart at him a second time, striking with wings and beak until both birds are tired of the sport, or the squirrel bolts to some place of refuge.

Robins and other thrushes are quick to drive away any gray squirrel that approaches the tree in which they are nesting, — an enmity which seems to show that this species is guilty of despoiling birds' nests; but there is no good evidence of this crime.   The red squirrel, however, is well

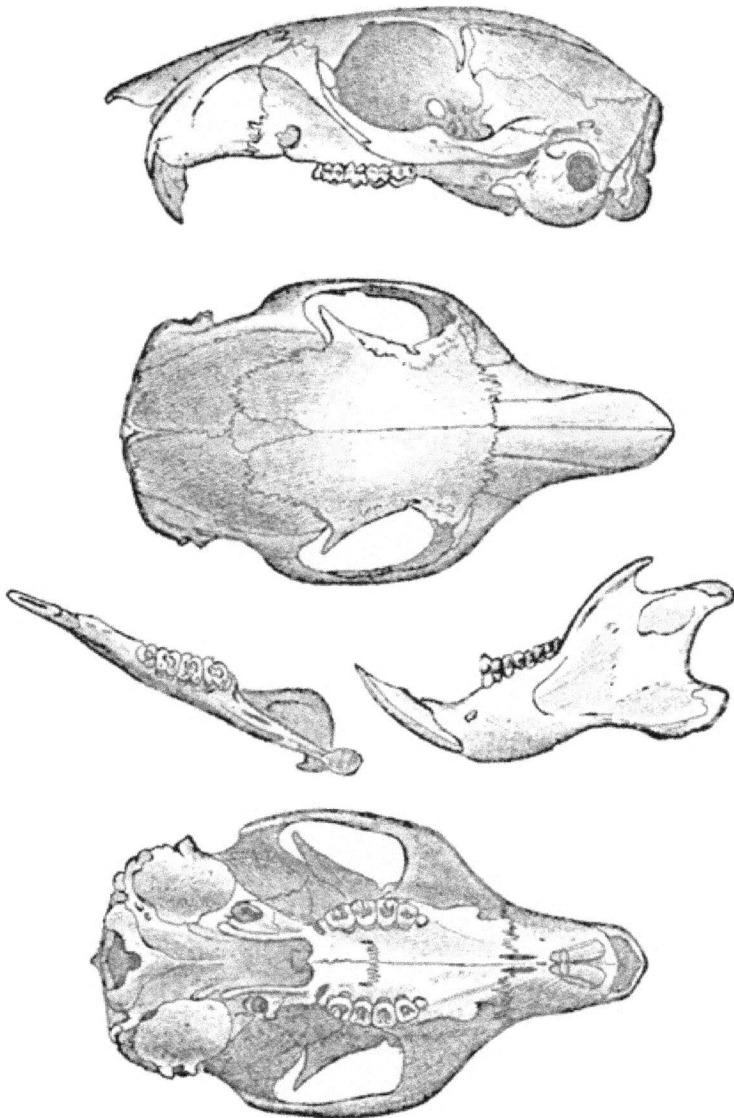

SKULL AND DENTITION OF A GRAY SQUIRREL.
Side view, upper and lower aspects, and lower jaw. — Natural size.
After Baird.

21

known as an incorrigible nest-robber and bird-
catcher, killing fledglings as well as sucking eggs:
sometimes, no doubt, his misdeeds have been laid
at the door of the innocent gray; and wise robins
take no chances. The flying-squirrel is likewise
overfond of birds' eggs.

In another point my observations were at vari-
ance with the books, which credit this squirrel
with somewhat nocturnal habits. Ours were often
abroad late into the dusk, and were out with the
dawn: but certainly they were never outside their
houses during the night, even in bright moonlight.
Merely wet weather does not daunt them, but a
heavy downpour of rain naturally drives them to
cover. They never take a water-bath, so far as
I know; but they are fond of rubbing and rolling
in loose sand, by way, I suppose, of ridding their
fur of vermin.

In winter they are more active, if possible, than
in summer, racing about the trees at a furious rate,
as if invigorated to fresh activity by the keen air.
Yet the book-writers insist that their habit is otherwise, and have described extensively their alleged
hibernation. Certainly our Connecticut squirrels
neither hibernate nor become torpid. During the
twenty-five years they have been under close observation here in New Haven there has never been
a day — excepting very sleety ones, perhaps —
when they did not appear.

The same denial must be made in respect to the

hoards of food reported laid up for winter use. Our grays store no " hoards " in the ordinary sense of the word, though both our red and our ground squirrels do so.

What the gray squirrels do is this : as soon as nuts and acorns begin to ripen in the autumn, they gather them with great industry, and bury them one by one, separately. They do this diligently and furtively, attracting no more attention than they can help. Hopping about in the grass until they have chosen a place, a hole, perhaps two inches deep, is hastily scraped out, the nut is pushed to the bottom and covered up. The animal then stamps down the earth and hurries away, hoping it has not been seen. They never bury the food given them or found in the summer, but in the fall will save and bury along with their wild provender the nuts and occasionally grains of corn taken from the window-sills.

Whether any of these are dug up before mid-winter I do not know ; I think not. The squirrels wander off into the woods when the mast is ripe, and get fat upon the oily food. But when this harvest is over, and their stores must be drawn upon, their ability in discovering them is wonderful. They seem to know precisely the spot in the grass where each nut is buried, and will go directly to it ; and I have seen them hundreds of times, when the snow was more than a foot deep, wade floundering through it straight to a certain point, dive down, perhaps clear out of sight, and in a moment emerge with the nut in their jaws.

Two hypotheses have been advanced in explanation of this unerring recovery of their treasures. One is that the animal remembers. But the difficulty of assuming this, under all the circumstances, is so great, that it seems easier to believe the alternative explanation, namely, that the treasure is found by aid of the sense of smell. It certainly seems to *us* that a hickory nut, after having been buried three or four months, and covered with a foot or two of snow, would be as unsmellable as anything could be; but it won't do to limit the sensitiveness of a squirrel's nose until we know more about it than we do at present.

At any rate, nearly, if not quite all, the nuts buried are exhumed before spring, for few hickory or oak saplings spring up in our grove, as would happen if any considerable number of seeds were left in the ground. Thoreau has a great deal to say on this topic in his suggestive essay on the Natural History of Massachusetts (in "Walden"), and credits the squirrels with doing an immense amount of tree-planting.

In confinement these squirrels will often attempt to bury nuts in the floor of their cages, going through the digging, covering, and patting motions as if the article were really buried. A writer in The American Naturalist for 1883 described this behavior on the part of a flying-squirrel which had been bred in the cage from babyhood, and thus must have acted purely under the impulse of inherited tendency or habit; moreover, this captive chose out of a large assortment only the acorns and hazel-nuts that grew wild in that locality, never attempting to bury peanuts, pecans, and other foreign fruits, although it ate them readily enough. Darwin, in his book on Earthworms, alludes to this practice, and uses it as an illustration of his doctrine that "the instincts of even the higher animals are often followed in a senseless or purposeless manner."

Our squirrels do not limit themselves to nuts, however. They are fond of buds, especially in the spring, devouring the maple and elm buds in particular; and in summer they feed largely on fungi and berries. Raspberries and strawberries please them especially well, and they are accused of choosing the biggest and ripest ones — a very sensible proceeding. They will eat dry kernels of Indian corn, if they are hungry, but delight in it when it is soft and milky, and in the early days of farming in the Western States, where the animals were very numerous, they committed depredations so serious that boys were set to patrol the field and drive them away. I am convinced that they also eat insects.

The ripening of the mast in the fall is the squirrel's gala-day, and the beginning of his work-day, too. He does not wait for the nuts to get ripe, but attacks their green husks, and his paws get richly stained with their brown juices. His powerful chisel-teeth quickly strip the shagbark nuts, but the clinging shucks of the pignut hickory are cut through. So rapidly does he work that a hard dry walnut will be opened and cleaned out in less than a minute. Those squirrels that inhabit coniferous forests subsist upon the seeds of the spruce and pine. These are procured by snipping off the scales, beginning at the butt end of the cone and following the spiral arrangement. They are also said by a writer in the Bulletin of the Nuttall Ornithological Club (VII, 54) to suck sap from certain trees.

Certain differences of size and coat noticeable between types of the North American gray squirrel from widely separated parts of the country, accompanied by local peculiarities of habit, led at first to the naming of several supposed species.

This doubt in the past as to specific unity well illustrates the principle that variations in size and color among all North American mammals and birds are correlated with geographical distribution, and seem to conform to varying conditions of climate. In general, it may be said that our animals show an enlargement of peripheral parts, that is, have longer limbs, tails, etc., in southern latitudes than toward the northern limits of their range; that the colors also increase in intensity southward; and third, that colors are more intense in regions of copious rainfall than in arid areas.

The squirrels exemplify these rules. In this species (*carolinensis*), for instance, a steady gradation may be detected from the light pure gray of the upper parts, characteristic of New England specimens, to the yellowish dorsal fur of the Florida type. In the fox-squirrels (*Sciurus niger*) of Wisconsin and Iowa the lower parts are only pale fulvous, in some specimens nearly white; about St. Louis they are strong, bright fulvous, and in lower Louisiana reddish fulvous or deep orange, while the back is far darker than northward. The same species fades westward from the bright specimens of the damp Mississippi Valley forests into a far paler variety along the dry edges of the Great Plains. The red squirrel (*S. hudsonius*) and the chipmunk (*Tamias striatus*) are also excellent illustrations of the action of climatic influences under this law — particularly the latter, whose color and stripes exhibited so many varieties between the Atlantic and Pacific coasts that early naturalists, having insufficient specimens, described confidently as several species what is now conceded to be only one.

The relative amount of moisture and shade seem to be the determining causes of this diversity, drouth and the blanching power of the sun in the high dry plains fading the pigments in the hair, or perhaps checking their deposition. The

effect of natural selection in adapting the animal
(in color) to its surroundings, by tending to make
it less conspicuous in an exposed than in a concealed habitat, is also to be considered here.

Quite distinct from this, however, seems to be
the tendency to melanism, which is so strongly
marked in several of our sciurids. Among flying-
squirrels, red squirrels, and chipmunks, a black
one is as rare as an albino — probably more rare ;
but in the cases of the gray and the fox squirrels
black examples are extremely common in some
parts of the country, and are popularly considered
a wholly separate species. But no such rule of
climate as mentioned above seems to control this
phenomenon, since black or dusky forms of both
species are as likely to be southern as northern in
their habitat. Where melanism occurs, it is likely
to prevail over a considerable district, sometimes
nearly if not quite to the exclusion of squirrels of
the normal tint. This shows that, though sporadic,
it "runs in families," descending from parents to
young ; yet not inevitably so, for many litters produced by black parents will contain a member or
two gray, or red, or grizzled, and black and normal
individuals mate freely. The "color-line" is not
drawn in sciurine society. Black ones, however,
are never, or very rarely, seen east of the Hudson
River ; and, furthermore, the northeastern black is
often rusty or brownish in tone, rather than pure,
especially in its summer pelage. Curiously enough

it was a specimen of this abnormal variety that first reached the hands of Linnæus, and consequently the specific name of the common fox-squirrel, normally vulpine red in color, as its name indicates, is *niger* — a fact that has led to much confusion in the minds of foreign writers upon American mammals.

A RED SQUIRREL.

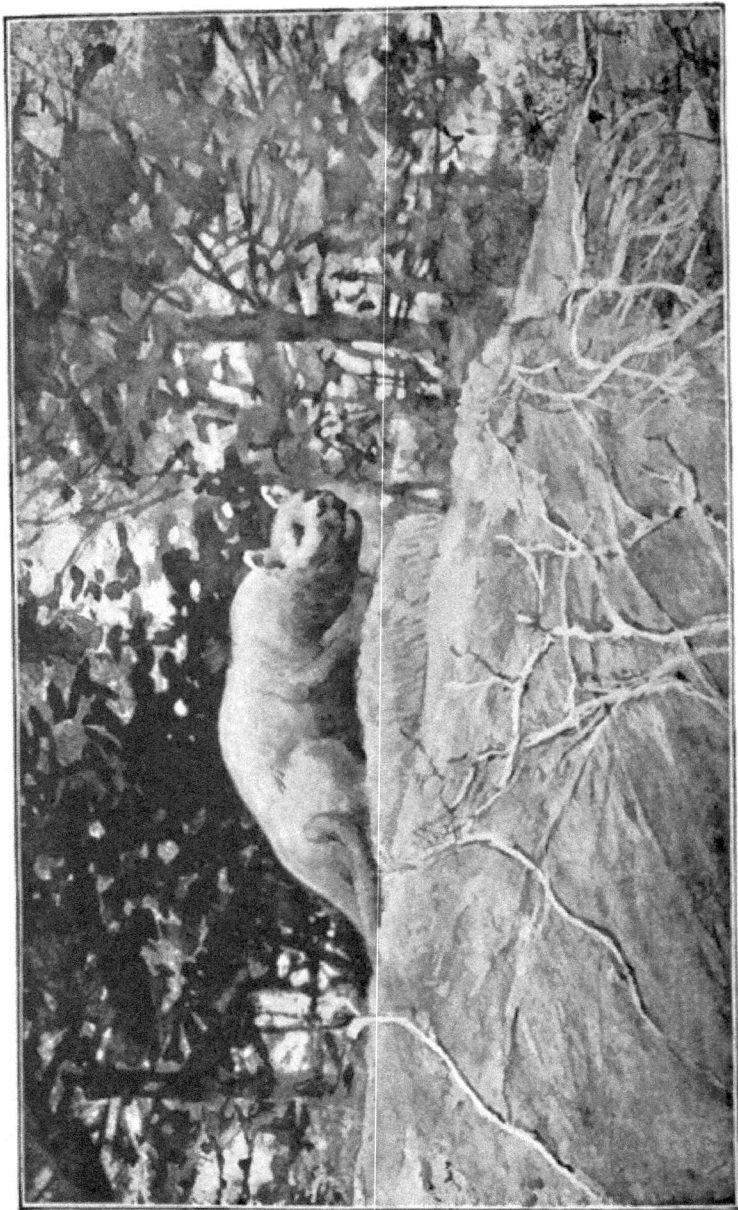

A PUMA IN BRONZE. — Kemeys's statue, "The Crouching Panther," in Central Park. New York.

32

II

THE FATHER OF GAME

I HAVE frequently noticed in menageries a start of surprise in the eyes of persons before a puma's cage, when they learned that this splendid cat was American.

It somehow informs our prosaic northern forests with a foreign, romantic, and adventurous spirit, to find such a denizen in them, for pictures of the lion, tiger, and leopard so fill our imaginations that all large and fierce beasts seem necessarily tropical. That, however, is by no means the fact. Even in America the jaguar wanders north to the Indian Territory — or once did — and south into Patagonia, while the puma is to be found from Canada to Cape Horn. Indeed, the wonder is that any natural barriers, less than wide spaces of water, restrict the range of these powerful animals. What prevented the jaguar, able to live along the western bank of the lower Mississippi, from spreading eastward, at least throughout the South Atlantic States? Yet we have no record that he ever did so, although "moving accidents of flood" must again and again have placed individuals and pairs on the eastern

shore of the Father of Waters, whose current the
jaguar is quite competent to swim, if he likes.   As
for the puma, he possesses the whole continent as
far north at least as the watershed of Hudson Bay,
in the east, while on the western coast he follows
the mountains to the middle of British Columbia.
Southward he is plentiful throughout the tropics,
and less so even to the Straits of Magellan.   No
other kind of cat, not only, but no other sort of
land animal whatever (not domesticated) equals
this species in north and south range (100 degrees); and that implies that no other is called
upon to adapt itself to such a diversity of seasons,
climatic conditions, food, and competition.   It has
to meet not only the cardinal contrasts of climate
between tropical and subarctic zones, but, as it is
widely distributed on both continents, it encounters
all the differences that can be found between life
in Canadian spruce-woods or on the high cordil-
leras from Alaska to Chile, and the moist, feverish
lowlands from the Mexican coasts to southern
Brazil.   One would expect to see in such a species
— the more so as the individual animals are not
far wanderers, but remarkably stationary in habitat — wide variations from the type; but, on the
contrary, few animals exhibit less diversity in size,
structure, or external appearance.

A comparison of the puma with the jaguar is
highly interesting in respect to color as well as in
the matter of distribution.   While the yellow hide

of the jaguar is adorned everywhere with black spots, the adult puma has no spots whatever, except that the lips are black, with a patch of white on each side of the muzzle, the outer rim of the ear is black, and sometimes the tip of the tail. Its upper parts are a uniform pale fox-red, more or less dull in certain lights, owing to the fact that each hair is fawn gray, red only at the tip; this color is more intense along the spine and decidedly lighter around the eyes, while the throat, belly, and inside of the legs are reddish white. The color is so much like that of the Virginia deer that their backs could hardly be distinguished at a little distance — in fact, precisely this mistake has been made by astonished hunters; and on the Amazons the puma is called "false deer." How helpful such a resemblance would prove to this wily beast, when stealing through the grass upon a herd of deer or any other prey that would have no reason to be alarmed by the known presence of what it took to be a deer, is at once evident.

The common term "American lion" goes back to the earliest days of European discovery on this continent, when the colonists supposed the hides the Indians brought in were those of the true lion, explaining the absence of maned examples by the theory that they had seen only female skins. "California lion," and "mountain lion," "red tiger," "panther" (or "painter"), are less excusable misnomers. "Puma" is said to be

Peruvian, and "cougar" is a shortening, through the French,[1] of a native Brazilian term; while "catamount," now rarely heard, is borrowed from Europe, and is confusing, because often applied to the lynx.

As everybody recognizes the advantage to the animal of the inconspicuousness of its plain reddish coat, and recalls at once the similar case of the lion, whose tawny hide harmonizes well with the sere grass of the South African karoo, or with the arid plains of the Sahara, Arabia, or Turkestan, it is customary to say hurriedly that this is the outcome of a beneficent process of natural selection. The same persons will tell you that the elaborate spotting of the jaguar is another striking example of the beneficence of the same law, acting within a different sphere, pointing out that the spots of its yellow hide harmonize so exactly with the dappling of the sunlight as it falls through the trembling leaves as to make the beast invisible to an unsuspecting eye. They may be right in these deductions, but there are certain difficulties in making the same rule apply to both, or, still more, to the case of the puma.

The jaguar confines his career to forests and

---

[1] Bates, in "The Naturalist on the Amazons," explains in a footnote on *sassú-ardna*, "false deer," that "the old zoölogist Marcgrave called the puma the cuguacurana, possibly (the *c*'s being soft or *ç*) a misspelling of *sassú-ardna;* hence the name couguar employed by French zoölogists." Alfred Russell Wallace ("Travels on the Amazon") spells it *sasurana* and attributes it to the Lingoa Geral.

swamps, among whose flickering lights his form is certainly easily lost to view, as also are those of the margay and ocelot, though the marblings of the latter are very different from the jaguar's sharp black rosettes; but unfortunately for the correlative half of the argument, the puma is also an inhabitant of the very same deep woods that are the home of the jaguar, ocelot, and margay in the south, and of the much-spotted lynx in the north; and so are the jaguarondi and eyra, neither of which have any variegations of hide to imitate the dapplings of light and shadow.

Another thing: We are told that the bold stripes of the Bengal tiger match so well with the vertical lights and shadows among the tall grasses and bamboos of an Indian jungle as to conceal that beast almost entirely when he lies within it; but a similar covert is a favorite lurking-place, along the River Plate, for our jaguar, yet he does not need, or at any rate does not possess, the vertical stripes regarded as indispensable to his East Indian cousin under the same circumstances.

When one surveys the whole family, he discovers that there are as many spotted cats on the plains and deserts as in the forests, and *vice versa;* and then, remembering that the habits of all are substantially the same, he begins to doubt the value of any conclusion in this direction drawn from one species. Moreover, it must not be forgotten that the cats are for the most part nocturnal animals, so that their color is of no great consequence, since the wisdom of the ages declares that "all cats are gray in the dark." The truth seems to be that there is a very forcible inherited tendency to spottedness in this family and its immediate allies, as the civets. In most members this persists in a remarkable degree, with interesting variations of pattern; while a minority have nearly outgrown it, and a few have lost the markings altogether, though even these, it should be noted, are born with spotted hides. There seems no reason to suppose that natural selection has had anything traceable to do with the origin of these markings, and but little to do with their modification or disappearance.

As to the size of the puma, one reads of specimens ten or eleven feet long; but no satisfactory evidence exists of a length greater than eight feet, measured from tip of nose to tip of tail, and the average will fall below seven feet. The jaguar has a longer and heavier body, but its tail is far shorter. Proportions vary somewhat, those from the tropics being a trifle larger than specimens taken in cool latitudes, following the law that an animal will reach its greatest size where the conditions are most favorable to its kind as a whole. The comparative fulness of the skull forward gives to the head a rounded solidity not usual in cats, and bears out the creature's reputation for craft. This gives to the face, also, an expression of intelligence quite different from the flat-headed, brutish, ferocity of many feline countenances. Yet, when the ears are laid flat back, the eyes half closed, the lips withdrawn in a snarl, and the animal crouched, with muscles tense and the corn-colored claws half-protruded, in readiness for a spring, its aspect is sufficiently terrifying.

This animal, nevertheless, is probably the most cowardly and least dangerous of all the larger carnivores. The South Americans dread it much less than the jaguar, and the Indians of our continent would far rather meet it than a bear. The instances are few where it has seriously resisted men when it could get away, and then it was almost invariably in defence of its young; and still fewer are the instances where it has made an unprovoked attack. One has often, it is true, approached a lone wood-chopper, or dogged the trail of a hunter or traveller through the wilderness, or prowled about some camp-fire or remote frontier cabin; but this behavior was evidently dictated in some cases by extreme hunger, but more often by mere curiosity and desire for company, and has been rarely followed by a harmful attack, though credible cases of its springing upon children have been recorded.

To this timidity is largely due the easy and early extinction of the beast in the eastern half of the Union, where, had it possessed the courage and power of resistance shown by the Old World leop-

ard and tiger, it might have remained to this day
a source of terror in many thinly settled neighbor-
hoods, such as the Catskill Mountains, which are
supposed to have been named in reference to it.
The rocky wilds of northeastern Quebec and New
Brunswick may shelter a few, and a small number
of pairs still survives in the Adirondacks, although
the bounty paid by the State since 1871 has nearly
exterminated them there. Ten years ago one
heard of an occasional panther in the Alleghanies,
and some probably remain in the swamps along
the western side of the lower Mississippi, and in
the Ozarks; but the whole northern-central region
of the Union has long been free from them. Practically, therefore, we may say that the puma has
disappeared east of the Black Hills and western
Texas; yet a century has not elapsed since one
was taken in Westchester County, N.Y., adjoining
New York City.

This animal seems never to have been very numerous — much less so than bears, wolves, or
lynxes. Nature, indeed, provides against undue
multiplication of these powerful and predatory
beasts. No machine with automatic governor,
however delicate, equals the self-acting influences
that preserve, in a state of nature, unbroken by
civilized interferences, the balance of an equal
chance for all — a true animal socialism. Thus a
single pair of these destructive and long-lived cats
seems originally to have occupied alone a certain

territory, the extent of which was determined by
their ability to hunt over it, and to defend it from
rivals of their own species, for they had nothing
else to fear.

It is an interesting speculation, indeed, whether
the apparent cowardice of the northern puma is
not in reality ignorance of danger, since he may
not suppose that man is more to be feared than
other large animals, whose attack he has no reason
to dread, even though, as in the case of the moose
and bison, he might hesitate to become himself the
attacking party. The conspicuously greater courage of the African and Asiatic cats might easily
have arisen from the need of frequently fighting
for their quarry with competitors as capable as
themselves, and from their constant encounters
with large and well-armed game, such as the rhi-
noceros, buffalo, and long-horned antelopes. Fierce
battles are reported, however, as occurring between
the California puma and grizzly bears.

It is not the habit of the puma to wander far
from the den, where a single family seems to make
its home. Whether a mate is taken for life is not
known, but at least it seems probable that a change
of partners is not made with each recurring season.
The male and female hunt separately, however, and
sportsmen assert that the latter is the better hunter
of the two. This, if true, is perhaps a result of
greater need and more constant practice, since she
must get food not only for herself, but for her

young, because the father does not summon his
family to share with him a feast, as the African
lion is said to do. The mother leads her half-
grown kittens about with her, and doubtless gives
them useful instruction; but, according to Merriam,
she leaves them somewhat behind when actually in
pursuit of prey, fetching them to share the results.

The amatory season occurs during the early winter (varying according to latitude and climate),
when the female's softened mood and desire for
companionship apparently lead her to strange
doings, for it is hard otherwise to account for the
actions related of certain cougars that have in-
sisted upon an unpleasantly close acquaintance
with, rather than have made an attack upon,
human beings. Thus several cases have been
related as occurring in broad daylight in the State
of Washington, where unarmed men or women
have been approached by a puma, which came
close, and even leaped upon them, knocking them
down and scaring them nearly to death, then retreated a little way, danced and rolled about, but
at first, at least, offered no harm, beyond playfully
seizing and tearing their clothes. Later, however,
a realization of human helplessness, together with
impatience at the lack of sympathy with feline
humor, sometimes provoked a more savage attack.

Nowhere is the puma more numerous and familiar, in spite of the war of extermination waged
against it by the ranchmen, than on the pampas

of southern Argentina; and it is interesting to read the following from "Gold Diggings at Cape Horn," by an excellent observer, John R. Spears, the most recent writer upon Patagonia:

"The lonely wayfarer is not often found there afoot, but men have been on the desert unmounted, and the panthers have come to play around them too. But it is not as a predatory cat that they come. It is as a playful kitten. Individual panthers play by themselves — old ones as well as young — by the hour. They will chase and paw and roll an upturned bush or a round rock or any moving thing, and lacking that will pretend to sneak up on an unwary game, crouching the while behind a bush or rock for concealment, to spring out at last and land on a hump of sand or a shadow. Then they turn round and do the same thing over again. When it is in this frame of mind, if a lone human being comes along, the panther is as glad to see him as a petted cat to see its mistress. It purrs and rolls over before him, and gallops from side to side, and makes no end of kitten-like motions, and all because of the exuberance of its youthful spirits. . . . The plainsmen of all Argentina call the panther by a name which means 'friend of man.'"

The young are born as early as February in Central America, where a second litter may occasionally be produced, as it is stated that kittens have been taken in August; but in the northern

United States the birth is considerably later. The period of gestation, according to observations in zoölogical gardens, varies from ninety-one to ninety-seven days. The kittens are brought forth among the mountains in some den beneath overhanging rocks; but in flat countries the mother secretes herself inside a dense thicket or cane-brake, where she prepares a bed of sticks and leaves. Four or five kittens may come at a birth, but usually only two or three; and Merriam thinks that in the East, at least, many more females are born than males. At first, as has been hinted, these kittens are covered with black spots and stripes, and the tail is ringed. Bonavia makes merry over the puzzled mind of the young father, when he beholds these varicolored offspring, and pictures the conjugal anxiety of the mother to convince her suspicious spouse that it is all right. The markings mostly disappear by the end of six months, but obscure reminders of them remain several months longer, and now and then are never quite outgrown. William A. Conklin, late keeper of the Central Park Menagerie, in New York, noted, from much experience with them, that the kittens opened their eyes after eight or nine days, cut their front teeth in eighteen or twenty days, and were weaned when three months old. The cubs do not become well-grown before the end of the second year, and during most of this time associate with the mother, who is valiant in their defence; and if we may

believe an account in that quaint old sportsmen's
magazine, " The Cabinet of Natural History," published in Philadelphia in 1830–31, of a deadly
attack by a cougar upon a bear, the explanation
is probably found in the fear of a mother that her
kittens were in danger.

Dr. Merriam concludes that in the Adirondacks
the puma breeds only once in two years.   If this
be true, it is a striking example of one of nature's
limitations of these destructive beasts, which would
seem, at first thought, to have a clear field for
indefinite multiplication.   But, though their food
is ordinarily abundant, no active enemies are to
be feared, and the climate holds no terrors, there
are certain insidious foes that they are powerless
to resist, in the form of parasites.   To these, and
especially to the internal sorts, the pumas, in common with other cats, seem to be peculiarly liable.   Various nematodes (thread-worms), trematodes
(flukes), and many kinds of tape-worms, are known
to attack this family.   Some of them grow in the
stomach and bowels, until the animal perishes of
exhaustion and starvation, while others penetrate
the lungs or liver, or encyst themselves among the
muscles, setting up there so fierce an inflammation
as to cause death unless (as doubtless often happens) the sufferer is sooner murdered by some
savage rival.   These parasites are taken into the
system from the living animals upon which the
cat feeds, especially from hares and other rodents.

This introduces the subject of the puma's food, which might be succinctly disposed of by the statement that he ate anything he could get his teeth upon in the way of flesh. As Spears picturesquely writes of it (in Patagonia): "It claws down the whirring partridge, as she springs from her nest, which it afterward robs of its eggs; it kills the ostrich as he sits on his nest, and then, after hiding his body, it returns to the nest and eats the eggs with gusto; it snatches the duck or the goose from its feeding-place at the edge of a lagoon; it crushes the shell of the waddling armadillo; it digs the mouse from its nest in the grass; it stalks the desert prairie-dog, and, dodging with easy motion the fangs of the serpent, it turns to claw and strip out its life before it can coil to strike again. The mainstay of his natural bill of fare in the North was the Virginia deer, especially fawns and yearlings, and in South America the guanaco."

Elks and moose could fight him off, as cattle are able to do, except when seized by surprise and from behind. In his admirable history of the quadrupeds of the Adirondacks, Dr. C. Hart Merriam gives the following lucid description of the cougar's method of hunting:

"Panthers hunt both day and night, but undoubtedly kill the larger part of their game after nightfall. When one scents a deer he leaps to the leeward and creeps stealthily toward it, as a cat does after a mouse. With noiseless tread and

crouching form does he pass over fallen trees and
ragged ledges, or through dense swamps and tangled thickets, till, if unobserved, within thirty or
forty feet of his intended victim. If he can now
attain a slight elevation and a firm footing, he
springs directly upon his prey, but if upon level
ground makes one or two preliminary leaps before
striking it. The noise thus made frightens the
deer, who makes a sudden and desperate effort to
escape. But, if lying down, several seconds are
necessary to get under full headway, and the panther follows so rapidly, in a series of successive
leaps, that it often succeeds in alighting on the
back of its unhappy quarry. Its long claws are
planted deep into the quivering flesh, and its sharp
teeth make quick work with the ill-fated sufferer.
If, however, the deer sees him in season, and can
get a good footing for a sudden move, it commonly
escapes, and the panther rarely follows it more
than a few rods, for as soon as he finds that the
deer is gaining on him he at once gives up the
chase. In fact, a panther rarely secures more
than one out of every four or five deer upon which
he attempts to spring. Then, too, it not infrequently happens that he strikes a deer when it is
under such headway that it escapes; and when
panthers were more plenty here than they now
are, it was no uncommon thing to shoot a deer
bearing deep scars upon its flanks — scars that
were clearly made by the claws of this powerful

beast. The female is by far the better hunter and does not lose so many deer as the male."

The puma by no means restricts himself to venison, however, and latterly has been able to get very little of it. He eats rabbits, ground-squirrels, and all the small animals that come in his way, including many sorts of birds, like partridges, that nest upon the ground. "Cougars are either particularly fond of porcupines," says Merriam, "or else are frequently forced by hunger to make a distasteful meal, for certain it is that large numbers of these beasts are destroyed by them. Indeed, it often happens that a panther is killed whose mouth and lips, and sometimes other parts also, fairly bristle with the quills of this formidable rodent." Even mice are not despised.

Like other cats it is fond of fish, and can sometimes catch them alive. Though not addicted to bathing, it is by no means afraid of the water. Dr. Suckley tells us that one exhibited for several years in San Francisco, a generation ago, was captured by being noosed from a steamboat, while swimming the Columbia River there, a mile and a half wide. Probably reptiles are not refused at a pinch, as the jaguar is known to eat iguanas, and to be fond of the crocodile, which it seizes and conquers in its native element. Insects and snails, even, do not come amiss. Carrion, however, seems never to be touched, though hunters agree that an animal lately killed by other hands, will be accepted, for instances are numerous where the panther has carried off not only deer that had been left out over night, but has taken game from before the very eyes of the sportsman. "One day," says Perry, "when shooting rabbits, I tied together a number that I had killed, and hung them on the branch of an alder which overhung the path. Returning along the same path shortly after, I met a cougar trotting leisurely along with my rabbits in his mouth. Having a shell loaded with buckshot, he paid for his dishonesty with his life."

The puma was quick to avail itself of the introduction of domestic cattle, and began to prey upon the settlers' pastures from the start. It has a particular *penchant* for horseflesh, and ravages the herds of Indian ponies on the plains and pampas, attacking first the colts, but often killing full-grown horses and mares. This may explain several recorded incidents of cougars leaping upon the horse of a traveller, but fleeing when they discovered the man in the saddle, even when, as usually happened, he had been dismounted by the plunging of the animal. The cougar probably failed to recognize the human being in that unaccustomed attitude, and was as much surprised as the man.

Calves, sheep, and hogs are also preyed upon ; and in the grazing districts of South America and our far West the cougars are yet so numerous, wherever a rough country offers them secure retreats, as to make a serious drawback in some

E

localities to profitable ranching. These forays happen as often by day as by night; and the deplorable feature of them is, that the marauder, with true brutish ferocity, is not content with satisfying his present hunger, but keeps on slashing right and left until he has struck down every animal within reach. Thus in many cases nineteen or twenty sheep have been slaughtered in a single foray, a little blood only being sucked from each one. The same story comes from the cattle, sheep, horse, and llama owners of South America, where, in the Andes, this animal abounds nearly up to the snow-line. Patagonian shepherds told Mr. Spears of losing from forty to one hundred and twenty sheep in a single night.

The manner of attack has been described, — a stealthy approach, followed by a lightning-like spring. The attempt, in the case of a large quadruped, is to knock it down with one blow of the muscular paw, then instantly to seize and pull back the head, breaking the neck; Darwin notes in his "Voyage," that he examined the skeletons of many llamas, said to have been killed by pumas, whose necks were dislocated in this manner. If that fails, a single bite of the long, lance-like, sectorial teeth on each side of the upper jaw, completes the work.

The quarry is not eaten on the spot, but is taken away to be devoured at leisure. Small animals are lifted free from the ground, but those as heavy as a calf or deer are dragged away into the bushes, the accounts in some books of its "flinging its prey over its back," and galloping away with it, being manifest exaggerations. Often he does not devour the flesh at once, or only begins upon it, then drags it away, covers it with leaves and brush, and waits to finish his meal when he is more hungry. When he has gorged himself, he retires a little distance and lies down to sleep. Hunters, knowing this habit, search the neighborhood of a "kill" as soon as they learn of one, sure that the puma is near by, and well aware that he is little to be feared in that state. Few men would be foolhardy enough to poke round in the brush in the hope of arousing a leopard from his after-dinner nap!

There is a widespread notion that the puma always lies in wait for prey upon the limbs of trees, and thence leaps upon its back. It appears that it may do — and has done — so in special places, as at the salt-licks of Kentucky, and at certain springs in Texas, where deer regularly came to drink, but certainly it is not a general, nor would it be a profitable, habit. Indeed, this animal shows a marked reluctance to climbing, rarely taking to trees except when pursued by a pack of peccaries, coyotes, or dogs, and then only for safety, and not as a point for advantageous attack. It frequently leaps from rocky elevations, however, and to an astonishing distance. Merriam says that on level ground a spring of twenty feet is by no means uncommon, and gives an account of one measuring sixty feet, where the cat leaped from a ledge twenty feet high and pushed the deer he struck a rod farther by the force of the impact. I have read somewhere of a pair known to have their lair on top of a rock that could be reached only by a vertical jump of twenty feet.

Their ordinary gait is a slouching walk or trot, and they are not swift of foot, except for a short succession of leaps. Otherwise, their movements have all that union of grace and quickness characteristic of cats.

The "blood-curdling screams" of the puma have furnished forth many a fine tale for the camp-fire, but evidence of this screaming, which will bear sober cross-examination, is scant. I myself have heard in the Rocky Mountains at night, shrill screams, so piercing and cat-like, yet of so much force and loudness, that it did not seem likely anything less than a cougar could utter them. I believed then, and am still of the opinion, that these were the cries of a puma: but I did not see the animal. Indeed, evidence so positive as this will be difficult to obtain, since loud yells are heard mainly at night, and would be unlikely to be emitted in the presence of a listener at any time. Says Mr. W. A. Perry, who has had a long personal acquaintance with these beasts, and in " The Big Game of North America " has written an excellent account of their habits in the Northwest:

"Sometimes, when the hunter is stalking the deer in the deep recesses of the forest, he is startled by a fiendish cry, — a cry so unearthly and so weird that even the man of stoutest heart will start in affright ; a cry that can only be likened to a scream of demoniac laughter. This is the cry of the male panther. If it is answered by the female, the response will be similar to the wail of a child in terrible pain."

To this may be added the testimony of Mr. W. A. Baillie-Grohman, one of the sanest and most trustworthy writers upon life in the Rocky Mountains, quoted from his excellent book " Camps in the Rockies " :

"Other strange sounds fall on the ear as I proceed with quickened step toward camp, sounds that you never hear in daytime, when, usually, oppressive stillness reigns in the great upland forests. The hoot of the owl is one of the most quaintly weird ; but it is not like the unearthly wail of the puma, or mountain-lion, demoniacal and ghoulish as no other sound in the wide realm of nature. As it re-echoes through the forests you involuntarily shudder, for it is more like a woman's long-drawn and piteous cry of terrible anguish than any other sound you could liken it to. Once heard, it will never be forgotten ; and it can no more be compared to the jabber of the coyote or the howl of the hyena, than a baby's cry of displeasure to its mother's piercing shriek as she sees the little one in a position of danger. Out only at night, they are of all beasts the most watchful, and most difficult to shoot; and, though their fearful call, in very close vicinity, has frequently stampeded our horses, and startled some of us from sleep, I have only been near enough to shoot, and kill, one single specimen in all my wanderings."

It does not appear, even here, however, that the writer had any better evidence than his "startled affright" in support of his assertion that the "fiendish cry" came from a cougar. In view of this uncertainty, some men go to the extreme of denying that any puma does or ever did utter such noises as have been described, saying that the story is a composition of fox-howl, screech-owl-hoot, imagination, and plain lying. This seems to me going too far. There is no reason why this animal should not caterwaul at times as well as its humbler relative of the back fence; and if we may be deceived for a moment, — as we sometimes are, — by Tom's or Julia's doleful wail, into thinking we hear a child in mortal pain, so we need not scoff unduly at those who hear in the naturally far louder caterwauling of the bigger cat-of-the-mountain, the agony of a man or woman under torture. Pumas do not shriek loudly in confinement, but they mew, whimper, and growl, like a house-cat, "only more so."

As winter approaches, the mountain lions de-

scend from their summer haunts in the higher
parts of the mountains and increase the number
in the valleys, — in other words, they follow the
game; and it is then that the rancher's herd suffers
most, and that in severe weather his corrals are
most often invaded.   Now and then a particular
panther is known to be the author of several successive outrages, and when he has been killed it is
usually found that he is an old fellow whose age
and worn teeth have put him behind in the competition of the woods, and led him to devote his
declining energies to the easier and safer raiding
of cattle and sheep.

At present the business of breeding horses and
donkeys in the mountain valleys of northern Mexico
is almost prevented by the prevalence of pumas.

When taken early, the kittens become interesting
and docile pets, as is frequently seen in South
America; but, as a rule, they become too treacherous and uncontrollable, with advancing age, to make
them safe companions.   It is, of the larger cats, the
one least frequently seen in the shows of animal-
trainers, although common in zoölogical gardens
and travelling menageries, where it breeds freely.

The hunting of the puma is hardly classed as a
sport in this country.   The Gauchos and aboriginal
nomads of Patagonia ride it down on horseback,
and kill it with their bolas or lances at short range.
Our Texan cow-boys occasionally meet one on the
prairie, and then have the fun of lassoing and

dragging it to death, unless they prefer to end its life with their six-shooters. The moment a lasso is round its neck it gives up, and even, it is said, "sheds tears, as if it knew and dreaded its fate."

In the Adirondacks, where they have been nearly exterminated to obtain the bounty ($20), they are hunted almost exclusively in winter, on snowshoes, the following of one often lasting several days. On the Pacific Coast, where many are poisoned, most of them are killed at an accidental meeting, a single ball, or even a charge of large shot, being usually sufficient for their quietus. Everywhere dogs are regarded as indispensable to success in regularly hunting them, — any sort of a cur will do.

Having reason to suspect the presence of a cougar, the hunter moves about until his dog goes away upon a scent, when he follows as best he can. It will not be long, usually, before the barking will tell him that his cur has discovered the quarry; and by the time he can overtake it he is pretty sure to find that the animal has taken to a tree, as this cat will almost invariably do as soon as it notices the approach of the dog, which seems to terrify it to a degree comical when we consider the difference in size. Many stories are told of how persons have supposed themselves saved from being torn to pieces by a puma by the courageous behavior of some small dog, that diverted the monster's attention. The jaguar, on the other hand, while hating a dog above all other creatures, is unterrified by it, and will do its best to catch and eat it. One shot usually ends the matter, but should the puma be wounded, but not crippled, it is likely to charge with tremendous force and fury, and become an exceedingly dangerous antagonist.

The hide is of no great value, though a favorite material among the Indians of the Southwest for bow and gun cases, perhaps with a half-superstitious idea that the skin of so mighty a hunter is peculiarly suited to such a purpose. The flesh (usually boiled) is eaten by all Indians, and is not despised by white men, since it is white and tender, with the taste and appearance, when roasted, of young pig. The fat of the panther is the most satisfying food of the Argentine desert, supplying the craving felt by the nomads of the Pampas for those nutritive elements elsewhere furnished by vegetable food, there so scarce.

Not many myths of the red men have clustered about this animal, despite its great size and strength, a fact perhaps due to the absence in it of attractive mental qualities. The cougar leaves little to the imagination. Clavigero's "History of Lower California" informs us that 150 years ago that province was so overrun with "lions" that the natives were kept in absolute subjection to the brutes, and were often glad to make a meal from the remains of their prey. This unchecked increase was owing to a superstition which prevented the Indians from killing a puma or even disturbing it

in any way, recalling the veneration felt and restraint exercised toward the tiger by certain sects
in India.   Dampier adds, subsequently, that the
Jesuit missionaries there were not able for a long
time to make any headway against this notion, and
could keep no live-stock in consequence.   Clans in
various tribes of the Southwest have been proudly
named after this successful hunter and model
guerilla ; and it stands at the head of the curious
" prey-god " theogony of the Zuñis, who call it the
" Father of Game."

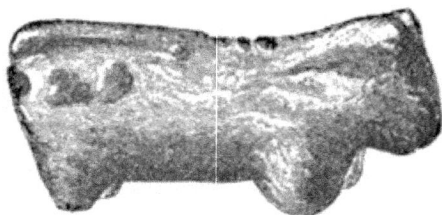

ZUÑI FETICHES OF THE PUMA.

60

THE SERVICE OF TAILS

A TAIL,[1] properly speaking, is a prolongation of the backbone behind (or beyond) the pelvic arch, which supports the hinder limbs.

Sometimes this prolongation is the larger half of the entire length of the spinal column, as in some reptiles and a few mammals, — the acme being reached by one of the African pangolins (*Manis tricuspis*), whose tail is nearly twice as long as its body, and contains forty-nine caudal vertebræ, the largest number known among mammals; sometimes it is extremely short, or altogether abortive, as among frogs and in our own case, for

[1] To the light-minded a better title would be *A Tale of Tails*, or something of that miserable sort — perhaps *A Caudal Lecture* — instead of the words at the head of the page. That would be a pun of the most brutal kind, as obvious and headlong as one of the bulls of Bashan. A pun should not come gradually bulging out towards one's intelligence — looming up slowly before the mind like a light-house in a fog. It should appear unexpectedly at your elbow, startling, yet not affrighting you, after the manner of the Cheshire Cat. Not on the lookout, you do not at once perceive the allusion, but an instant later the essence of wit encased in the quibble declares itself, as certain candies, disappointing and flavorless at first, presently disclose a liquid centre of sweets to the surprised palate.

even humanity possesses the rudiment of a tail concealed beneath the skin. The same is true of the more human-like kinds of monkeys (the apes).

Some tails, like those of the bear, deer, and goat, are so short, stubbed, and immovable as to defy any attempt to perceive a present purpose in their existence. Of what possible use to a turtle, for example, is its tail? None, apparently, whatever might have been the case in the differently constituted ancestors of the turtle. This part has simply remained after its service in chelonian economy had been long outgrown, as buttons are still sewed upon the sleeves of our coats, although a century has elapsed since men thus fastened back their too voluminous cuffs.

It is a survival of the misfit.

Indeed, it would not be easy, were one to insist upon visible utility in every case, to prove the serviceability of some of the most pretentious of these appendages. Look at the wild cats. The panther and the ocelot have long and graceful tails; the lynxes own the merest apology for one, and are irreverently dubbed "bobcats" in the West. Yet you cannot say that the former species thrives better than the latter. Length or brevity of tail seems to have nothing to do with either habits or happiness. Thus the wrens and our various thrashers (Harporhynchi) are cousins-german; yet the wren's tail is an absurd little tuft of short feathers "weel cockit" over his rump, and that of the thrasher is long and drooping. The brilliant sun-birds and gaudy parrots content themselves with short rectrices, while the no less ornamented humming-birds and trogons of our tropical woods trail behind them plumes of vivid color, often three times as long as the body.

Sometimes the tail carries out the general contour of the body, and its origin is scarcely discernible, externally, as among snakes and most fishes; again, it is an almost naked appendage, as among the rats; while a third class can be made of tails plentifully furnished, and, as a rule, highly adorned, with hair or feathers, such as those of the horse, the squirrels, the ant-eater, the fox, the malodorous skunk, and the gorgeous peacock,[1] pheasants and birds-of-paradise.

But a more interesting line of inquiry is to trace the manifold ways in which wild animals turn their tails to practical account. These appendages are as a fifth limb to a great number of creatures who would be sadly deficient without them. They serve their various owners as shelters; as garments; as receptacles, carriers, and tools; as respirators; as badges for friend or foe; as weapons, both for offence and defence; as anchors, supports and aids to locomotion on land as well as under the water and through the air; as musical instruments (for example, by the rattlesnake), or as a means

---

[1] In this bird, however, the resplendent train really consists of tail-coverts and not of the *rectrices*, or true tail-feathers.

of expression in a great variety of gestures; as matrimonial advertisements; as egg-holders and incubators; and finally, as baby carriages, — for in all these ways do tails enter into the ministry of limbs to one or another animal.

And here it is well to broaden out the word "tail" so as to include more posterior appendages than are included in my first strict definition. Nevertheless, we must draw the line inside of popular usage even here. The prolongations of the wings of certain butterflies, for instance, are not "tails," though entomologists term them so in a special sense; nor would it be allowable to include the spinnerets of spiders, nor the stings of bees, nor the ovipositors of many insects, although these sometimes extend in hair-like tubes beyond the tip of the abdomen, nor the apparently similar breathing-tubes of the Ranatra bugs.

But it is right to speak of the "tail" of the scorpion-fly (Panorpa), — which is articulated exactly like that of a scorpion, — of the skip-jack beetle, and of a few other insects; while the word is fairly applied to certain worms, to all the swimming crabs, the cuttle-fishes, and even to gasteropod mollusks, wherever the body is lengthened out into a more or less serviceable hinder part.

Let us take up some of these utilities in their order and illustrate them. What animals, to begin with, employ their tails as a shelter? Well, the great ant-eater does so, for one. The tail of the

ant-eater is an enormous brush, which he is said
to bend over his body like an umbrella. His
home is in the Amazonian forests, where tremendous rains fall; and as it is his business to be abroad
in the forest, pushing his way through the dripping undergrowth at all hours, such an umbrella,
as Mr. Wallace assures us, is of great service
to him, — except when it gets him into trouble.
This usually hap-
pens by reason of
an Indian's rat-
tling the leaves

THE GREAT ANT-EATER.

in imitation of a
shower, and taking
advantage of the
poor beast's haste to elevate his umbrella, to rush
forward and kill it. Hence the wisest of the ant-
eaters have concluded that there are times when it
is well to know enough *not* to go in when it rains.

The long and ample tail-feathers of East Indian
pheasants form a pent-house, with sloping roofs
beneath which the chicks huddle, warm and dry

F

during showers, — a habit especially illustrated in
the Himalayan peacock-pheasants (Polyplectron),
whose young spend most of their time beneath
the shelter and concealment of their mother's fan-
like tail, coming out only when called to pick up
the food she scratches out of the leaves. Here
the tail is a nursery.

As for the hermit-crabs, while one could not say
they make a shelter of their tails, it is certain that
they could not obtain and hold the shell-homes
with which they provide themselves, and that are
necessary to their existence, were it not for their
ability to hold on to them by means of their flexible tails, which grasp the inner whorls, and form
an effective lease of the premises.

As for garments, — who that ever has seen a
squirrel humped up on a cold day with its tail
pressed close along its back; or a raccoon, a fox,
or a cat, sitting with its feet wrapped in the furry
" boa " of its tail, can doubt that this is the putting
on of an overcoat? Only warmly furred animals,
by the way, have bushy tails; and all these sleep
curled up, with the tail around the face as birds
place their heads beneath their wings. As such
animals usually sleep alone, they need more protection against an undue loss of heat while asleep
than do animals that take their repose huddled
together in groups that warm one another; hence
their blanket-like tails. An attendant benefit of
sinking the nose into the brush, as Mr. Law-

son Tait has pointed out, is that it answers the purpose of a respirator, warming the air, before it is breathed, to a temperature more suitable for health, and one that will detract less heat from the body than would air entering the lungs wholly untempered.

An extension of this overcoat idea into that of a coat of mail is exhibited in certain of the armadillos, as the tatusids, where the scaly investiture of the long tail is a part of the protection of the soft under-parts when the animal rolls itself into a ball and defies its enemy's teeth. The same is true of the larger pangolins, whose tail, covered with scales on the outside, and held closely appressed to its rolled-up body, is a very important part of its self-protection. In that excellent book, William T. Hornaday's "Two Years in the Jungle," you may read a most instructive account of the Indian species of pangolin (*Manis pentadac-tyla*), a live example of which was kept by the author for some time, as follows:

"My new pet evidently expected fair treatment at our hands, for he soon uncoiled himself and stood up for examination. He was just three feet long, including his tail, — which by itself measured seventeen inches, — and his weight was eighteen pounds. This tail was a most useful appendage, for it was very broad, measuring five and a half inches across where it joined the body, slightly hollowed underneath and rounded on the top, its official purpose being to protect the animal's head. In walking, he carried his back very highly arched in the middle, and . . . his heavy tail barely cleared the ground. . . .

"If ever a small animal was especially created to resist the attacks of destroyers, that manis must have been the one. In such plate-armor as he wore he could roll himself up and defy the teeth of the jackal, or leopard, or the fangs of the cobra. Having no teeth at all, and claws fashioned only for digging, he would have fared badly in the jungle without his defensive coat of mail. From the tip of his nose to the tip of his tail he was covered with broad, flattened, shield-shaped plates of clear, gray horn. . . .

"Not having any one to introduce me, I undertook to get along without that formality; but it was of no use. He immediately tucked his head down between his fore legs, brought his tail under his body and up over his head, and held it there, forming of himself a flattened ball completely covered with scales.

"I said to him, 'My fine fellow, I really must insist upon knowing you more intimately; so here goes.'

"I then undertook to uncoil him, but found I could not accomplish the task alone. I called Henrique to help me, but the tail stuck to the body, as if it had been riveted there.

"I also called Canis to help, and while I held

the body, the other two braced themselves against me and pulled on the tail with all their strength, to uncoil it. We wrestled with it until we were fairly exhausted, failed utterly, and gave up beaten. Such was the wonderful power in the tail of that small animal."

As a receptacle and carrier of eggs the tail parts of certain among the lower animals serve an important purpose in their economy. In the lobster, and its miniature, the fresh-water crayfish, the latter segments of the abdomen form a fan-shaped tail, on the under surface of which are small appendages called swimmerets. When the eggs have ripened between the ovaries of the female (whose swimmerets are especially adapted to their purpose, and different from those of the male), they are extruded from openings in the second pair of legs, just back of the great front claws. These eggs are covered with a viscid matter, something like those of the frog, which is readily drawn out into threads. These threads become entangled with the hairs covering the swimmerets, and thus several hundreds of eggs attach themselves to each swimmeret, and appear as large grape-like bunches, filling the whole space beneath the tail. Here they develop under the most favorable conditions, and after the young have hatched, these hold on to the swimmerets, and are carried about and protected by the mother until they are able to care for themselves. Here is another caudal nursery.

Perhaps this is as good a place as any to speak of one of the most comical uses to which a tail is put—that in the opossum family. Here the rat-like, wiry tail is decidedly prehensile—a feature to be spoken of later. The opossum uses it constantly to grasp the limbs and assist her climbing and holding on. When her young are large enough to go out with her, which is soon after they are born, she endeavors to lead or carry them through the tree-tops, and struggles to climb about the branches, and make use of her prehensile tail as she is accustomed to do; but she often finds that member of no use, for eight or ten squeaking little brats, miniatures of herself, are digging their sharp toes into her fur and clinging with their own tails tightly twisted around hers, which is curved over her back to form a hand-rail for the young crew. If one lets go of this convenient member, it is only to take a convulsive half-hitch around some twig, and thus anchor the whole company, or to choke the poor mother by a twist around her throat or impede her movements by a death-like grasp of one or more of her legs. The same useful member—a fifth hand, as it has often been called— enables baby monkeys of the prehensile-tailed South American kinds, to cling to the mothers in their almost aerial flights through the tree-tops.

The use of its tail as a *tool* (distinguished from a weapon) is common enough in the animal kingdom, without going into the region of fable for instances, as the old writers used to do when they told how the beaver brought mud and laid it, mason-like, with his tail for a trowel. If this member has any part in the beaver's architecture, it is only by the accidental slaps and rubs it may give to the muddy structure as the animal swims around it. The scaly, vertically compressed, knife-like tail of the muskrat would be much better adapted to such a service, but the muskrat puts little or no mud into its house building. What the stout, scaly, spatulate tail of the beaver really does do, is to serve as a powerful sculling oar and rudder in swimming and diving; and the same is true of the muskrat.

One of the most curious features of that curious creature, the king-crab, or horse-foot, of our sea-shores, is the flexibly jointed, bayonet-like spine which forms its tail, and has no analogue elsewhere among crustaceans. He only acquires it as he ap-

A HORSE-SHOE CRAB, USING ITS TAIL (TELSON) AS A LEVER.

proaches adult age, so that it is, as Lockwood expresses it, "a sword of honor," betokening the end of youth. Whether or not this sharp rapier is of value as a weapon nobody seems to know, but it certainly makes a capital alpenstock. The horse-foot is light, and is liable, by the least agitation of the water, to be turned on its back, when it would be as helpless as a tortoise but for this sharp spike, the point of which it deflects and forces into the sand, thus lifting its hinder parts, and enabling it to roll over upon its feet again. Moreover, were it not for this natural leaping-pole, which is planted firmly in her rear as a brace, the female horse-foot would be unable to push her carapace into the sand, and thus make the burrow which she requires for her eggs.

Many of the smaller, bivalved mollusks, or "shell-fish," of sandy ocean-shores are persistent burrowers, and all delve tail foremost. The common soft clam is a good example. Here the pointed, pliable tip of the body, which may be called its tail, is the tool used; and on page 159 of my "Country Cousins,"[1] the way in which the operation is cleverly performed by the pretty little Donax, or wedge-shell, is fully explained.

The adroitness with which animals have caught fish with their tails as lures and sometimes as lines, forms the theme of many a barbaric legend and myth. The Norse people say that the bear once had a long tail, but under the advice of the fox, who was jealous of bruin's rivalry in the matter of caudal adornment, he lowered it through a hole in the ice as a fish-line, and held it there

---

[1] Country Cousins. Short Studies in the Natural History of the United States. By Ernest Ingersoll. Pages 252. Illustrated. Square 8vo. Harper & Brothers, New York, 1884. Cloth, $2.50.

until it froze in, and its discomfited owner could get away only by breaking it off — mighty near its root, as any one can see to this day. This story, paralleled elsewhere in folk-lore, is an amusing fancy; but one might imagine a monkey really able to do something of that kind, if any monkey could be found which cared for fish.

An actual instance, however, is afforded by the fish-eating bat of Trinidad (*Noctilio leporinus*), which finds its tail, and the membranes that connect that appendage with the thighs, of eminent service to it. Observers in the Trinidad Field Naturalists' Club report (see their Journal, Vol. I, page 204) that this bat catches its prey (a fish) by throwing it up with the interfemoral membrane. Simultaneously the bat bends its head toward its tail to seize the fish as it is thrown from the water. Probably its long, sharp, curved toe-nails are also of assistance in this queer method of fishing.

Similarly, ingenious rats have been known to purloin oil, jelly, and such desirable liquids from bottles too narrow for their entrance, by inserting their tails, and then licking the dripping member, or giving it to a neighbor to lick. Professor George J. Romanes proved beyond question that they did so, by experiments which are detailed in his book, "Animal Intelligence," to which the reader is referred.

A like utilization of resources is the strategy of the puma, as observed on the Patagonian pampas,

where he lies flat down within view of a herd of
guanacos that are feeding towards him, and holding up the end of his tail (which is nearly black)
lets it tremble there.   It is sure to attract the attention of the animals, who are certain to approach,
led by curiosity, near enough to give the big cat a
certain capture of one if not more of their number.

The tails of creatures that swim or fly perform
a very important service in these methods of locomotion; while in many cases this is a helpful or
even indispensable member in progression upon
land.   The tremendous leaps of the minute skip-
jack beetles, and of the agile sand-fleas, are made
by springing from the bent hinder parts of their
body, and not by leg-force, as in the cases of the
grasshopper and true fleas.   Certain fishes, like
the file-fish, are accustomed to poise themselves
upon their tails, almost motionless, for long periods, when it is well-nigh impossible to distinguish
one of them from the ribbons of the eel-grass in
the midst of which they dwell; while the eels and
many serpents are able to stand erect upon almost
the very tip of the tail, or to hang thereby, and
some can even spring off from it, if we may believe the statement of Professor Owen, though I
do not know of any snake quite so acrobatic.

It is related in the older books of natural history
that the kangaroo sits, when reared up, upon his
massive tail and strong hind limbs, as upon a tripod; and that it is by the elastic force of the tail

that it is enabled to make its long, running leaps,
which, in the case of the large wallaby, will average eight or ten yards at each jump. This is now
known to be largely an error; the truth (as shown
by its tracks in the mud and by careful observation) is, that the tail only just touches the ground
now and then; yet it is plain that this heavy member serves a useful purpose in balancing the creature. The same must
have been true of those
vast reptiles of the
Mesozoic days, the
dinosaurs, whose

THE JERBOA
KANGAROO.

tracks are
impressed so plen-
tifully upon the
brownstone rocks
of the Connecticut
valley, and of similar animals, in other parts of the
ancient world, known to have had enormous caudal
parts — a characteristic of primitive forms.

One very distinct service the tail of one modern
marsupial may perform, is illustrated in the behavior of the jerboa kangaroo, which collects the

grass for its nest and takes it home in a bundle or thick wisp, grasped in the curled-up extremity of its strongly prehensile tail. Gould illustrates this in his monograph on the Macropodidæ; and remarks that, "as may be easily imagined, their appearance, when leaping toward their nests with their tails loaded with grasses, is exceedingly amusing."

Referring again, for a moment, to the suggestion that the tail in the large wallabies, and creatures of similar proportions, is useful as a balancing-pole, it may be added that a similar explanation has been offered for the long tails that characterize most of the mice, especially those like the zapus and jerboa that are powerful leapers; at any rate, the service of a balancing-pole is unquestionably performed by the tails of many climbing and jumping mammals, and by all birds, as can be well seen in the act of alighting. As for the tufts common at the ends of many of the long-tailed mice, etc., it has been said that that was an extra advantage in the same direction, comparable to the string of knotted papers that boys attach to their kites.

Another quaint explanation of the tufted and brush-tipped tails will be noticed farther on.

To many tree-haunting animals, such as the opossum, the South American forest monkeys, and some others, the tail has been modified into a most effective instrument for grasping and holding on, even in sleep, by the acquirement of what is called *prehensibility* in its tip, similar to that in the toes of perching-birds, which close tightly around a twig, without any effort on the bird's part, simply as the result of the pressure of its weight.

Charles Waterton points out that this faculty is of manifest advantage to the animal, either when sitting in repose on the branch of a tree or during its journey onward through the gloomy recesses of the wilderness. "You may see this monkey," he writes, "catching hold of the branches with its hands, and at the same time twisting its tail around one of them, as if in want of additional support; and this prehensile tail is sufficiently strong to hold the animal in its place, even when all its four limbs are detached from the tree, so that it can swing to and fro, and amuse itself, solely through the instrumentality of its prehensile tail — which, by the way, would be of no manner of use to it did accident or misfortune force the monkey to take up a temporary abode upon the ground. For several inches from its extremity, by nature and by constant use, this tail has assumed somewhat the appearance of the inside of a man's finger, entirely denuded of hair or fur underneath, but not so on the upper part."

Prehensibility is equally well developed in the naked, rat-like tail of the 'possum of our Northern woods, and to a less extent in the manis; in the Old World, or true, chameleon; in the tips of the tails of tree-clinging serpents; and among fishes it exists perfectly in the quaint little sea-horse (Hippocampus), which is a poor swimmer, and rests by hooking its tail around a bit of sea-weed or coral, or through a hole in a broken shell, thus anchoring itself securely.

A service of the same nature is performed by the tail of many birds that are accustomed to climb about the trunks of trees, and cling to upright rocks, etc., instead of walking on the ground or perching upon the branches. Familiar examples are the woodpeckers, nuthatches, creeping-

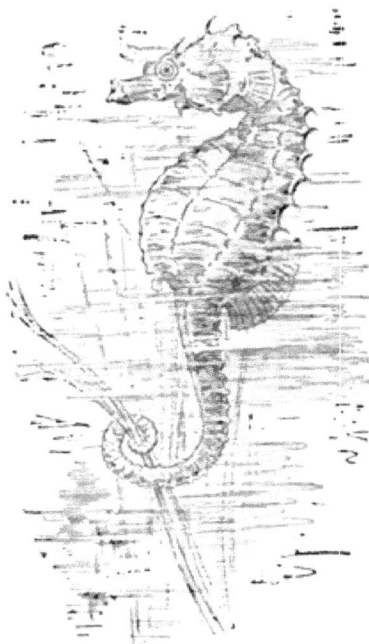

PREHENSILE TAIL OF THE SEA-HORSE.

wrens (Certhiadæ), and swifts. Whenever these birds rest a moment they press the tail hard against the bark or other surface to which they cling with muscular toes, and lean upon it. Such a leverage is very important to enable the woodpeckers and nuthatches to deliver their sturdy and repeated blows; and without such a support the swift could hardly hold itself, as it does for long periods, at rest

against the wall of a hollow tree, rock-crevice, or
chimney. As a result, the end of the tail-feathers
of such birds has become stiffened and capable of
this special work to a remarkable degree; while in
the case of the common chimney swift, and some
similar, rock-climbing species of
the East, the shafts of the
feathers project beyond the
vanes in long, sharp spines,
equal in effect to the climbing-
irons of a telegraph lineman.

Among animals that live in
the water, the tail becomes of
supreme importance in locomotion. The shrimp's swimming is wholly by reaching its
tail out and pulling itself back-

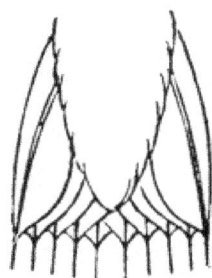

SPINES TERMINATING
THE TAIL-QUILLS
OF A SWIFT.

ward. This, of course, is the principle of the oar;
and the shrimp is able to "feather," since the
plates of his tail shut up like a fan in recovering
for a new stroke.

It is mainly as a screw-propeller, however, that
their tails serve the swimmers — precisely the motion a man makes when sculling a boat by a single
oar held over the stern. This motion is plainly
visible in fishes, the most swift and powerful among
which have the smallest body-fins; and it is solely
by this sculling movement of the tail that the shark
and bluefish make such terrific rushes after prey,
that the trout is able to give the angler so much

work, and the salmon to climb or leap up water-
falls, the ascent of which excites our amazement.
Alligators, crocodiles, and aquatic lizards, such as
those of India and Egypt, have little other means
of progress under water, yet they are powerful
swimmers; the Nile monitor, in fact, can swim
much faster than young crocodiles of its own size,
of which it captures and devours large numbers,
by reason of the vertical flattening of its tail.
The profound diving of a whale, the follow-my-
leader bounding play of the porpoise and dolphin,
and the impetus for soaring gained by the flying-
fish, are all due to the propulsion of the tail, the
principle of which is embodied in the two-bladed
propellers of our swift steamships. Even some of
the diving-birds make their way under the surface
by closing their wings and sculling the short and
stiff feathers of the tail, though other diving-birds
paddle with their wings under the water just as
they fly in the air.

In all these flying and swimming creatures, not
only birds and fishes, but the marine mammals and
the flying quadrupeds, the tail is a rudder, as well
as a propeller and balance. This is easily observable not only in the flight of any bird, but in that of
the flying and leaping squirrels; and no doubt it
is an essential part of the apparatus for flight possessed by these animals, — including the checking
and controlling of the speed, as observation of a
bird passing or alighting will quickly show; while

the same observation may prove true of winged insects having hinder appendages or prolonged abdomens, such as dragon-flies. "Short-tailed birds," remarks Frank M. Chapman, "generally fly in a straight course, and cannot make sharp turns, while long-tailed birds can pursue a most erratic course with marvellous ease and grace. The grebes are practically tailless, and their flight is comparatively direct, but the swallow-tailed kite, with a tail a foot or more in length, can dash to right or left at the most abrupt angle."

Many a wild creature trusts to its tail for defence in time of danger, and finds in it an offensive as well as a defensive weapon of no mean worth. The "fighting formation" of the American porcupine, for instance,[1] is to turn its back on its foe, hide its head beneath its thorny neck, and strike right and left with its short, spade-shaped tail: this organ is armed with the longest and strongest spines, and it is astonishing what a quick, forcible, and effective blow the little animal can thus deliver. It is probable that the heavy, knobbed tail of the gigantic Mesozoic glyptodon was similarly used. Whales will stave a boat to pieces by a stroke with their powerful flukes; and the "thresher" shark takes his name from his habit of swinging violently back and forth the long scythe-like prolongation of the upper half of his tail-fin. It is said that he kills small fishes for his

[1] See also Chapter VII, page 188.

G

prey by thus thrashing about in a school of them, and that several of these sharks, combining in their attack, will beat a whale to death; but there is little evidence of the truth of either assertion.

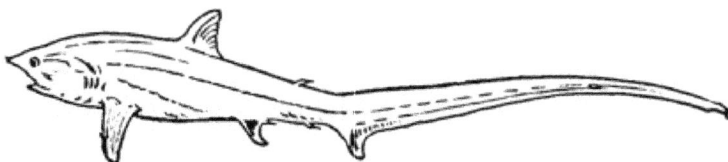

THE THRESHER SHARK.

As for crocodiles and alligators, although their dreadful jaws are their principal weapon, the blow one of these great saurians can give, when he "swings the scaly horror of his folded tail," is justly to be dreaded by anything it may come into contact with. How serviceable this member may be to the East African crocodile, for instance, appears from the narrative of Dr. J. W. Gregory, the author of "The Great Rift Valley," who relates his experience with them on the Tana River as follows:

"The animals are surprised when asleep on the bank, and killed with spears; but the work is rather dangerous, and inexperienced men are frequently knocked over by a blow from the reptile's tail, and dragged into the river. . . . I was once fishing in the river Ngatana, from a bank about six feet above it, when the chief came and warned me not to sit so near the water, as a crocodile might knock me into it by a blow with his tail. . . .

Later on, I found that the natives of other Pokomo
villages attribute the same power to the crocodile,
and the German missionaries at Ngao knew of
cases where people had been thus swept into the
river and killed.   The natives on the Nile told
Sir Samuel Baker the same story, and it is hardly
likely that it would have been independently in-
vented in two such distant localities, and by such
different tribes, if it had no basis in fact."

Of course if a man, then an antelope, or fish-
seeking cat, or any other animal of similar size,
could be knocked into the stream and preyed
upon; and that this must often happen is manifest from the great numbers of these reptiles which
inhabit streams too small to furnish sufficient food
in the way of fishes alone.

The same habit belongs to the lesser land-lizards,
all of which whip severely with their tails when
fighting, large ones, like the South American
teguexin, being able to keep dogs at a distance by their fear of these blows; and it is
said that in their quarrels most lizards seek first
of all to disable the opponent's tail, success in
which manœuvre wins the battle.   This seems to
be a trifling casualty in the case of many species,
such as the geckos, and some American lizards,
whose tails break off on the slightest provocation,
sometimes, apparently, as a wilful stratagem on
the creature's part, of which a good example
is found in the behavior of the very common

ground-lizard of the Southern States (*Oligosoma laterale*), as described by Mr. H. C. Bumpus and others:

"If captured, — a by no means easy task, — they make no violent effort to escape, but, with a most droll expression, they eye their captor; soon winning his confidence, but betraying it at the most unexpected moment, for with a quick struggle the tail is dropped off, and, before one has recovered from his surprise, no lizard is to be seen, the tail only remaining, which for some little time twists about with as much vigor as when attached to its owner.

"The self-mutilation of the lizard offers a remarkable instance of protection," comments Mr. Bumpus. "It will be seen that the animal, being comparatively slow of foot, cannot ordinarily seek safety in flight, and having no organs of defence, it, on being attacked, breaks off a portion of its tail, which, still alive and twisting about by reflex action, attracts the attention of the enemy, and the lizard, unencumbered and unnoticed, glides into some crevice and is safe.

"The muscles of the tail are so arranged that they, by contraction, close over the place of amputation, and bleeding is prevented. From the thus blunted appendage a new rudiment soon appears, which, in a short time, replaces the lost part."

Now this is all matter of fact, and true of several

other lizards;[1] and I have no disposition to deny
the practical service it is to the species possessing
such brittle tails, on the principle that a man thanks
his stars for the fire-escape that enables him to save
his life even at the expense of all his property : but
some of the darwinizing it has received is beyond
my following, at any rate. Mr. Poulton, for instance, reasons that the very length of the tail is
a protective product of natural selection, it having
been so increased for the express purpose of
making it easier for an enemy to seize it, and thus
more surely fail (by reason of its breaking off) to
catch the body of the lizard; we are told that
"tails" on the wings of certain butterflies are made
conspicuous for a like reason. Then Mr. Poulton
goes on to argue further that the long tails characteristic of most mice, and especially of the many
species which have a racket-shaped or brush-like
tuft of hair at the end, are due to the same influence : and, furthermore, that an explanation of the
bushy tails of the squirrel, fox, wolf, jackal, etc.,
is contained in the same protective hypothesis.

---

[1] It is also true of a small snail in the Philippines, whose "tail"
(properly the hinder end of its body or foot) will break off if seized :
as it is more highly colored than any other part, it is the most conspicuous point for seizure, but the bird or lizard that takes hold
there gets nothing but a wriggling tip for his pains, while the snail
drops to the ground and hides. Semper, who expounds this doctrine at length, says that he lost specimens frequently by trying to
pick them up by their tails ; and that ten per cent. of these snails
(Helicarion) showed the scar of a previous loss.

Now from appearances alone one might build up a pretty bit of logical fancy-work like this, but habits as well as structure must be considered, — use as well as shape. Otherwise we shall make the mistake of the birds who sit on telegraph wires and point out to one another the beneficence of humanity, which has considerately provided them with perches: and how, in beautiful adaptation, the perches are most extensive and numerous precisely in those cleared and cultivated parts of the country where the birds are in greatest number and most in need of such conveniences!

Let us look at the matter from the side of actual habits. In the first place, we notice that many of the long-tailed lizards (and some among them having the most whip-like tails) are not provided with the detachable arrangement, at all, so that in their case the slenderness and length of this appendage must be due to other causes; while, on the other hand, many lizards have very short and stubbed tails, yet seem to thrive as well. Next, of all the natural enemies of the lizard only one kind — the snakes — might be supposed to creep upon them from the rear, and hence seize the extended tail first; and these would be obliged to let go later, and take a new hold of their prey, in order to profit by it, — a movement which would set the quick lizard free in ninety-nine cases out of a hundred. A snake must swallow this or any large animal headforemost, and always endeavors to seize

it by the head, because the ordinary serpent having
once seized a victim never lets go until he has
swallowed it. Lastly, there is no observable difference, so far as this point is concerned, between
the behavior of those lizards with long brittle tails
and those with firm tails or scarcely any tail at all;
and the most brittle one of all, the "glass snake,"
so called, is a subterranean species that rarely ex-
poses either end of its body to capture.

As to the mice, they do not ordinarily carry their
tails in an extended position, but almost invariably
keep them curled about their feet, as if they were
afraid something might bite them, instead of anxious to induce a possible foe to seize them, in order
that they might jerk them out of his clutch and
laugh at his discomfiture at finding only a mouth-
ful of fur instead of a fat morsel in his teeth. No
mouse or squirrel is fool enough for that; and if
by accident, the situation is ever created, no pursuer is fool enough to sit still and curse his luck
while the mutilated mouse or squirrel ambles gaily
away. Moreover, there are short-tailed mice. With
such bushy-tailed quadrupeds as the wolves, jackals, and foxes, the case is still worse for the argument. The very last thing such an animal does,
when in danger, is to straighten out his tail. His
first impulse, on the contrary, is to tuck it as far
between his hind legs as he can. The very hardest part for an enemy to seize would be its bushy
tail, and the worst; for instantly the head would

fly around, and, finding the attacker engaged, would have an advantage in a fight for life which no wild animal would ever allow another. Who ever heard of a fox saving himself by yielding his brush, as Siberian travellers are said to throw mittens, children, and the like, to bears that chase their sledges. The fact is, that about all of a fox which remains uninjured, and is preservable as a trophy, after the huntsman's pack has pulled him down, is his brush, in which the dogs take no interest.

If, instead of this wild escapade in evolution the writer quoted had devoted himself to showing that the short tail of most of the deer, antelopes and goats, and of rabbits and burrowing rodents, which are regularly chased by swift-footed canine beasts, was due to the gradual reduction of this appendage through natural selection, because length was a disadvantage in bulk and otherwise, without corresponding service, he might have made an argument both credible and interesting. These animals are pursued by the carnivora, which, when overtaking them, *might* seize a long tail, as they would have nothing to fear from their jaws. As a matter of fact this often happens to wild cattle, as used to be illustrated on our western plains — the foremost wolf of the pack fastening himself to the buffalo's tail, and dragging back until its companions had reached and seized the nose and flanks of the retarded animal. It might be adduced in support of this that the tails of the horse, zebra, and other equines, and such large horse-like antelopes as the gnus, had remained long, and often really bushy, because these animals were kickers, and able to prevent with their heels any attempt to bite this long appendage. A natural corollary of this would be the fact that the secretive habits of the mice, which live in holes, are mainly nocturnal, and are attacked by large animals only by being pounced upon or dug out, rendered the length of their tails neither helpful nor harmful to them so far as enemies are concerned; having probably no more to do with their means of defence than have their large ears — nor so much !

Let us, after this digression, return to the main line of our story, and ascertain further how certain of these appendages serve as weapons, and are even armed to that end.

In the geological long-ago there lived flying saurians with long tails; and one of these, described by Professor Marsh, had spines two feet long on the side of its tail, running outward and backward.

A fish more unpleasant to meet than even this long-departed animal is well known along our Eastern coast, as well as in many other parts of the world, under the name of sting-ray, or stingaree. The rays (or skates) are flat, triangular-shaped brutes, allied to the sharks in structure; and they have slender, whiplash-like tails. That of the stingaree (which sometimes reaches a length of ten feet) bears upon its top, near the root, a long, sharp and barbed spine, with which it is able to inflict deep and dangerous wounds, when aroused to self-defence. Some acrid or poisonous substance seems to enter the lacerations thus made, and fishermen pierced in the feet or hands by this species, or by the tropical whip-ray, as often happens, find their wounds slow and painful in healing.

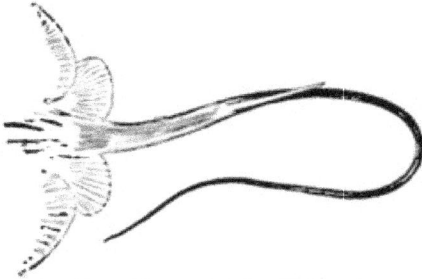

ARMED TAIL OF THE STING-RAY.

Something of the same kind, but even worse, is the stabbing apparatus of the surgeon-fish of Florida and the West Indies. "Each side of the tail," says Goode, "is provided with a sharp, lancet-like spine, which, when at rest, is received into a sheath, but it may be thrust out at right angles to the body, and used as a weapon of offence; sweeping the tail from side to side as they swim, they can inflict very serious wounds, and I have seen in the Bermudas large fishes, confined in the same aquarium-tank with them, covered with gashes inflicted in this manner."

In the philosophy of animal coloring brought about by natural selection, which has been elaborated by Alfred Russell Wallace, Mr. Poulton, and

others, a prominent part is often assigned to the tail
as a badge of identity, especially among mammals
and birds. In many species of mammals it is conspicuously colored above, but is white underneath,
in which case it is likely to be carried erect.
Deer, goats, and certain antelopes are good examples; and their white cocked-up tails are the
most noticeable part of them as they flee away,
forming an unmistakable mark to guide their
companions whose safety lies in keeping in a close
herd. Our common little gray rabbit, or "Molly
Cotton-tail," is another good example; and a still
more striking one is afforded by the skunk, as is
explained in the chapter on that interesting animal. Such badges are called "recognition colors";
and their primary purpose — if the correctness of
the theory be conceded — is to bring the sexes
together. I have spoken of tails of this conspicuous sort as serving the purpose of marriage-
advertisements to their wearers.

This term applies even more exactly to the
adornments of the tail (or tail coverts) of many
birds, such as are seen in the resplendent fan of
the peacock, the immensely long and exquisitely
ocellated trains of the argus and other oriental
pheasants, the lustrous expanse of the wild turkey,
and in many other large birds, which display these
ornaments to their fullest extent, while they pose
and strut before the females to attract their
preference. But there are many smaller birds in

which the tail-feathers are greatly prolonged, modified and highly ornamented in the males, apparently for the same purpose. Such, for example, are the trogons, and particularly Guatemala's national bird, the quesal, which opens and curls and displays the long emerald plumes that descend from his tail in a most magnificent manner for the benefit of his plainly dressed mate. How curious are the tails of some birds of paradise! The humming-birds offer similar examples: but here it is the curious shape of a pair or so of prolonged rectrices rather than their color; and one may guess a reason for this when he watches a hummer on the wing, for so exceedingly rapid is the movement of the wings as it poises before a flower, or in front of its demure little mate, that it seems only a jewel flaming in a mist of scintillant light. No particular ornament or pattern of color is or could be visible, but above it, raised and steady, are the long tail-feathers, straight, curved, emarginate, thread-like or variously racketed, which declare its identity like a badge to the knowing eyes of the other bird. These are standards — recognition marks — in shape as well as color; and they signal the language of courtship at the same time, — an ornithological flirtation.

A reminder of facts like these — especially as regards the mammals — called forth recently some suggestive remarks from Dr. E. Bonavia, of England, as follows:

" As regards the white tip of the tail of certain mammals, there are some curious phenomena connected with tips. . . . White and black are interchangeable. There are many mammals which have black tips to their tails, and this, in allied or other individuals, may change to white. The Arctic hare in its summer dress is brown with black tips to his ears; and the ermine is also brown with half the tip end of the tail black. When these two animals get their snow-white winter clothing the tips of the ears of the one, and the tip of the tail of the other, remain black."

These peculiarities of color may be correlated with the fact that the tips of ears, occasionally, and the tips of tails, very frequently, are adorned with tufts of hair, in the case of animals not otherwise long-furred. That is the case with all the hoofed beasts that have long tails, as the horses and asses, cattle, camels, giraffe, and several of the South African antelopes; the practical service of this as a wisp to drive away biting insects is recognized by every one; and it results in the ability of such animals to stay on the plains all summer, while their short-tailed relatives are obliged to migrate to mountain-tops and other regions of sometimes poorer pasturage in order to escape the flies.

This phenomenon of marked color and increased hairiness at " tips " may be further correlated with the fact that in the tip of the tail, particularly, seems to be centred or focalized, an unusual degree of nervous force, or sensitiveness, or both, which induces an extra supply of nutrition or stimulus at that point to the pigment or hair cells, or both, — for it must be noted that terminal tufts of hair are likely to be strongly colored, as, for example, in the lion, puma, and giraffe. If this is so, it furnishes an explanation of the tufted condition of the tails of so many mice, for which doubtless the animal has a use of its own, — very likely as a balancing pole or weight; and so natural selection

A JERBOA, SHOWING TUFTED TAIL.

has had an intimate structural basis upon which to bring about modifications in each species beneficial to it "after its kind."

How much outward evidence there is of extreme nervousness in the tip of the tail — not to refer now to the expressive mobility of the whole member as manifested by dogs — will be plain to any one who will watch a collection of cats in a menagerie. Even when they are in repose, the dark end of the tail seems to be involuntarily curling and twisting, like the head of an uneasy serpent; and are they aroused, this agitation becomes very marked indeed. I do not suppose that the puma which lies in wait for the guanacos, and attracts them by his lifted tail as hunters sometimes toll up the pronghorn by lying on their faces and kicking up their heels, thought that strategy out and put it into deliberate execution; but the waving of the tail was practically involuntary, and he has learned to adapt his hunting to a method whose success *we* can explain, but which he probably never has fathomed or sought to fathom, for that matter.

Serpents give a conspicuous example of this nervous condition of the tail. Every snake, when excited, elevates the tip of it, which is highly sensitive to touch, and vibrates it with more or less rapidity. This is most marked in the viperine species, and it is here that we find the horny tips, and the rattles of the rattlesnake, which can be agitated with such extreme rapidity as to make merely a fan of light — the eye cannot follow the motion — and can be sustained for hours. There is good reason to believe that the presence of the rattle is connected with, if not the result of, this maximum nervousness. How great the importance of this is in the economy of this kind of serpent, and the way in which it is important, I have endeavored to show elsewhere.[1] The rattling of the

---

[1] " Rattlesnakes in Fact and Fancy," — Chapter IX of my book "Country Cousins," published by Harper & Brothers, New York, 1884.

quills of the tail of the European porcupine, under circumstances of alarm, is another interesting fact discussed in Chapter VII.

But the large part the tail plays in the expression of brute emotions, from furious anger to extravagant joy, is familiar to most persons and need not be dwelt upon here. Mr. Darwin has treated of it extensively in his capital book "The Expression of the Emotions." Foxes, wolves, jackals, *et id omne genus*, exhibit excitement and alarm by elevating or depressing their brushes, and no doubt wag them in welcome to their friends. The nervous organization and moral sensitiveness of dogs have been greatly enhanced by their long association with man, and domestic dogs have many more emotions to express, no doubt, than their wild, or semi-wild, congeners. I have been struck by the lack of affectionate demonstrativeness among the yelping and often savage dogs about an Indian camp. It was rare that any of them were made pets of, and they had never been led to show that welcome and gratitude and joy which are so plainly expressed by the flexible tails of the terriers, and poodles, and collies of our houses.

A FAMILY OF COYOTES.

From a photograph of a mounted group in the National Museum at Washington

THE HOUND OF THE PLAINS

A PICTURE of the Great Plains is incomplete without a coyote or two hurrying furtively through the distance. The coyote is a wolf, about two-thirds the size of the well-known European species represented in North America by the big gray or timber-wolf. He has a long lean body, legs a trifle short, but sinewy and active; a head more fox-like than wolfish, for the nose is long and pointed; yellow eyes set in spectacle-frames of black eyelids; and hanging, tan-trimmed ears that may be erected, giving a well-merited air of alertness to their wearer; a tail (straight as a pointer's) also fox-like, for it is bushy beyond the ordinary lupine type; and a shaggy, large-maned, wind-ruffled, dust-gathering coat of dingy white, suffused with tawny brown, or often decidedly brindled.

> "Blown out of the prairie in twilight and dew,
> Half bold and half timid, yet lazy all through,
>
> * * * * *
>
> Lop-eared and large-jointed, but ever, alway,
> A thoroughly vagabond outcast in gray."

Such is the coyote : *genus loci* of the plains : an Ishmaelite of the desert : consort of rattlesnake and vulture : the tyrant of his inferiors : the jackal of the puma : once a hanger-on upon the flanks of the buffalo herds, and now the pest of the cattlemen and sheep herders : the pariah of his own race, and despised by mankind.

Withal, he maintains himself, and his tribe increases. He outstrips animals fleeter than himself. He foils those of far greater strength than his own. He excels all rivals in cunning and intelligence. He furnishes the Indian with a breed of domestic dogs, and makes an interesting exhibit in menageries and trick-shows.

The coyote is little known at present east of the bunch-grass plains. In early days, however, he was common enough in the open country of Arkansas, Missouri, Illinois, and northward, whence he received the names "prairie-wolf," "red" and "barking" wolf. Threading the passes regardless of altitude, he wanders among all the foothills of the complicated mountain-system that forms the "crest of the continent," and dwells too plentifully in the Californian valleys, thriving upon what he can pilfer from the ranch-yards and corrals, and on the young calves or lambs that he is now and then able to steal from the flock. Hence he there passes his life continually on guard against guns, traps, and poison.

In the United States and the Canadian North-

west, then, he is a creature of the open country,
leaving high mountains and forested regions to
the large gray "mountain" or "timber" wolf
(*Canis lupus*).   Perhaps this is less his choice than
his necessity, for in Mexico and Central America
he seeks his food more often in forests than elsewhere, yet keeps his characteristic cunning and
cowardice, becoming there the wild dog of the
jungles, as in the north he is the hound of the
plains.   It is that tropical region, indeed, which
gives us his name, for "coyote" comes from the
pure Nahuatl word *coyotl*, the final *l* softened into
an *e*.   This ultimate must not be lost in the pronun-
ciation, which is coy-o'te, in three syllables, — not
ki-yōt, as often heard.   The word is translated in
the old Nahuatl-Spanish dictionaries by the Spanish *adibe*, a term applied to the African jackals.
It is also employed as a terminal of generic signifi-
cation for all similar animals, as Dr. Daniel G.
Brinton has explained.   Thus *tlal-coyotl*, from
tlalli, earth, and *coyotl*, is a big burrowing animal
found in Mexico.   The derivation of *coyotl*, indeed,
appears to be from the root *coy-*, which means a
hole, alluding, of course, to the burrowing habits.
I have met, in an indigenous Californian language,
a very similar word which is said to mean "hill-
dog."

When this wolf cannot find a natural hollow in
the earth to suit him, nor evict some unhappy
hare, prairie-dog, or badger, he digs for himself a

dry burrow, or prepares a den among loose rocks. The *butte* districts of the upper Missouri and lower Colorado valleys are therefore his strong-holds. There the decay of sandstone strata, and the breakage due to volcanic eruptions and upheavals, give him the choice of a large number of crannies, while the desolation and remoteness of wide tracts untenanted by men still afford him the seclusion he covets.

In such seclusion his young family of from five to eight pups is brought forth during the latter part of spring, the date varying with the latitude. It is just before and after the birth of the puppies that the old dog-coyotes work their hardest and the most systematically. In hunting at this time our wolf adds to his ordinary pertinacity and zeal, the sagacity and endurance necessary to turn his victims and drive them back as near as possible to his home, knowing that otherwise his mate and her weaklings will be unable to partake of the feast.

A remarkable picture of this was given some years ago in an English magazine (unfortunately I have lost the exact reference) by a traveller who, in one of the best "animal chapters" it has ever been my privilege to read, detailed a chase of this kind as witnessed by him in the grand forests near Lake Nicaragua.

The traveller and his Indian hunter-companion had discovered, just before encamping for the night, that a band of coyotes was on the hunt in the neighborhood; and were aroused before daylight next morning by the sudden outburst from their clamorous throats.

"Their musical cry, reckless and unguarded now, resounded from hill to hill, and echoed in the deep forest. All at once it burst upon the ear, as if some messenger from the front had just arrived. Past the lower ridge, down the forest to our left, swept the pack, each hound seeming to rival the other in noisy glee. Across the wind they galloped, and the rising gusts bore to us that cheery music long after they had passed far away through the long glades and green savannahs."

It is plain that an Englishman wrote that paragraph. No one but a fox-hunter could take and communicate such enjoyment from a chorus of wolfish notes.

Expecting their return, the hunter placed himself at sunrise on a ridge overlooking Lake Nicaragua, and makes us envy him by his description of the scene, "of a grandeur and variety and loveliness," he exclaims, "not to be surpassed in any Eden of the world."

"At length," he continues, "I fancied the breeze brought a faint clamor, as of dogs upon the scent. Five minutes more and a tall buck, his coat all staring and wet, his tongue hanging low, bounded across a rocky stream choked with big-leaved plants, which intersected one of the glades within my sight.

He vanished in the forest. And now there was no possibility of mistake. The distant cry of the pack came each instant louder to the ear; at top speed they swept along the trail, heads up high and bushy tails waving. They followed over the stream without a check, and disappeared under the arches of the wood. Presently I heard the crashing of undergrowth and threw myself flat upon the ground. Laboring terribly, the buck broke cover at the foot of the ridge, and ran along the forest on my left. The coyotes' triumphant cry rang louder and louder, and then they, too, appeared, running as fresh as at the beginning of the chase. They dashed along in a compact mass, eight or ten couple of grown dogs, and toiling after were three or four heavy bitches, and a dozen sturdy pups of all ages: these had plainly joined the chase only a few moments before, for they were playing and biting one another.

" I rose to my feet and watched with the greatest interest, for it seemed certain that the buck must have over-run the coyotes' trail and his own scent. My guess was correct. On the edge of the forest, a big old dog which had led the pack, raised his muzzle and howled. Each hound stood still, and then I could mark that some of the finest animals were much more blown than the others, thus showing that the game had been turned by a forced gallop. The leader sniffed about for a moment, then uttered a sharp whine, on which the pack

opened like a fan, while the whelps sank far into
the rear. Scarcely had the last dog vanished in
the undergrowth, nose and tail to earth, when a
short challenge rang out. There was a moment's
pause, while the old dogs verified the fact, I suppose. A bolder cry proclaimed that all was well,
and the pups, which had been standing still as
statues in their place, dashed off into the wood.
Then the music of the pack broke out again; they
swept away under the mysterious trees and I saw
them no more.

"Certainly," exclaimed the narrator, at the conclusion of this brilliant and instructive story, "no
training could have bettered that day's run. To
drive a grown buck back to his starting-place; to
send on a portion of the pack to that point where
he would strive to break cover; to head him again
and again into the covert, where his speed could
not be exerted to the full, were facts which might
puzzle all the best dogs in England, and the human
intelligence which directs them."

His game and its getting are not always so noble
as this, however, and the coyote knows well the
pinch of famine, especially in winter. It has been
remarked that the main object of his life seems
to be the satisfying of a hunger which is always
craving; and to this aim all his cunning, impu-
dence, and audacity are mainly directed. Nothing comes amiss. Though by no means the
swiftest-footed quadruped upon the plains, he runs

down the deer, pronghorn, and others, tiring them out by trickery and overcoming them by numbers. The buffalo formerly afforded him an unfailing supply in the way of carrion and fragments left by his Brahmins,—the timber-wolves,—who steadily followed the herds and seized upon decrepit or aged stragglers, and upon any calves that they were able to "cut out" and pull down. In such piracy the coyotes themselves engaged whenever they saw an opportunity, although it tried their highest powers; and success, when attained, followed a system of tireless and sanguinary worrying. The poor bison or elk upon which they concentrated might trample and gore half the pack, but the rest would stay by him and finally nag him to exhaustion and death.

I remember once reading an account of the strategy by which a large stag was forced to succumb to a pack that had driven it upon the ice of a frozen lake, as they had deliberately planned to do. Part of the wolves then formed a circle about the pond, within which the slipping and exhausted deer was chased round and round by patrols, frequently relieved, until, fainting with fatigue and loss of blood, the noble animal fell, to be torn to pieces in an instant.

Far less worthy game attracts him, however. In California and New Mexico he has become so destructive to the sheep that incessant war is waged upon him by the ranchmen. In Kansas and Nebraska he is accused of making havoc among the domestic poultry, but it is quite likely he gets the discredit of many depredations by foxes, weasels, and skunks. Similar misdeeds were justly charged against him by the farmers of Illinois and Wisconsin, when, fifty years ago, the prairies of those States were the frontier. Two or three times a year, therefore, a general holiday would be declared, and a wolf-hunt organized, in which volunteers from all the surrounding settlements would gather, form a circle miles in diameter around the spot to which the game was to be driven, and then, systematically marching forward, would concentrate until they had corralled the animals into a small district. Such battues would result in the destruction of great numbers not only of prairie-wolves, but also of lynxes, polecats, and other "vermin," and free the neighborhood of these pests for that season at least, besides being the occasion of a social merrymaking rare enough to be keenly enjoyed among the frontiersmen.

Tactics similar to those in coursing a stag upon the ice, as already mentioned, are pursued by the coyote when he sets his heart upon a hare. Alone, he could neither overtake nor surprise it. Two wolves assist one another, therefore, one giving instant chase while the other squats upon his haunches and watches the operation. The runner turns the hare in a circle that presently brings it back near to the point of starting, where the second wolf is ready to keep puss going while the first rests. Then the wolf in chase bowls the hare over, and seeks to appropriate the whole of his not over-big carcass before the resting partner can come up and claim his share, whereupon a row is very likely to ensue.

To capture the sage-hen, grouse, or quail, the coyote roughly quarters the ground, somewhat like a trained dog, but with frequent crouching pauses, all the time wending his way toward the quarry. At the right moment he will drop flat in the grass and creep stealthily forward, as a cat would do, until near enough to make a fatal spring. The birds do not seem to lie to him as they will to a setter or pointer, but get up and fly the instant they discover his presence.

In fact, nothing edible escapes this omnivorous prowler. It is the arch-enemy of such small deer as prairie-dogs and gophers; and one reason why the rabbits have become such a pest in central California is that this wolf has been mercilessly killed off there.

If no better food offers, it will revel in carrion of any sort. "It resorts in great numbers to the vicinity of settlements where offal is sure to be found, and surrounds the hunter's camp at night. It is well known to follow for days in the trail of a traveller's party, and each morning, just after camp is broken, it rushes in to claim whatever eatable refuse may have been left behind. But it cannot always find a sufficiency of animal food. Particularly in the fall, it feeds extensively on 'tuñas,' which are the juicy, soft, scarlet fruit of various species of prickly pear (*opuntia*); and in the winter upon berries of various sorts, particularly those of the juniper."

Under the pangs of excessive hunger these small wolves are compelled to a furtive boldness of which they are incapable under ordinary circumstances. Thus I have known them to come repeatedly within pistol-range of my camp-fire in southern Colorado, and hunters tell me that they have been known to pull, or try to pull, the boots or the leather straps of a saddle, from under the head of a slumbering camper. Sitgreaves records that when, for two days and nights, his party had kept possession of some solitary springs in an arid part of Arizona, the coyotes became so desperate from thirst that they would come to drink while men and mules were at the spring.

In the account of their habits in Nicaragua, to which I have already referred, is included the opinion of the Indian who was accompanying the writer, and who evidently held this wolf in higher respect than do those of us who know the animal only on the plains.

" You see [says Manuelo] they are not like other beasts, afraid of fire. . . . They cluster round it at night, and the larger your fire, the more coyotes.

Ay! there's cause for fear when one is alone and the pack is out. They're worse then than tigers or the cowardly pumas, though there are few who believe it. They come sneaking up through the black glades, noiseless and silent, and they squat on their haunches and their eyes shine like stars. They wait and watch and will not be driven off. You shoot one, but others come. They sit like ghosts — like pale devils — round your fire. Ah! I tell you, señor, it is terrible to be beset by coyotes!

"Hour by hour they sit there, just out of reach, in a circle around you. It is a nightmare! From very weariness you doze off, and, waking with a horrid start, you shout to see how near the devils have crept. As you spring up, they slink back again, and take the former ring, licking their foxy jaws, but making no sound. And you — you rush at them; and they glide away and vanish on the instant in the black undergrowth. But, as you return, they come forth again, they sit down, and stare with never a wink in their green eyes. It is terrible, señor!"

As a rule, on our western plains, they are cowardly to the last degree, and trust to superior numbers and well-laid plans to effect their object. I remember at a place where I once encamped for two or three days in southwestern Wyoming, the rough ledge of a butte-face, just across the creek, was the home of a family of these wolves, and I often saw them, — the mother lying at the mouth of her den, and the four whelps romping in the sunshine. The father of this family kept out of sight, but the second day I caught sight of him in pursuit of a doe antelope and her fawn.

The doe was backing away on the plain, keeping the little one, who seemed to understand its part perfectly, close to her hind legs. Following her closely was the wolf, frequently making a dash to the right or left, to get at the fawn, but each time the brave little mother, whirling alertly, would present to him her lowered head, and make a dash at his skull with her sharp fore hoofs. Thus she retreated; but I fear that the pursuer's longer breath and varied tactics won the day at last. It is said that this wolf can even kill the rattlesnake, by sheer quickness of onslaught.

A prime characteristic of the coyote is his astonishing voice, which differs so much from the well-known wolfish howl of other members of his race as to have suggested the specific name *Canis latrans*, or barking wolf. It begins with a series of sharp yelps which quickly run into a prolonged howl that may strike you as dismal or simply interesting — hardly alarming — as you happen to feel. Often these yelps and howls are repeated with such rapidity and ventriloquistic force, as to seem to fill the whole horizon, and the unsophisticated traveller will be certain a large pack is near him, when in fact the whole clamor is raised by one, or at most two, lean and hungry barkers.

Remembering these astonishing vocal performances, it is amusing to read the story told by the
Kaibabits Indians, of northern Arizona, to account
for the diversity of languages, for what animal
could better figure in such a history?

The old men of the Kaibabits say, the grandmother goddess of all brought up out of the sea a
sack, which she gave to the Cin-au'-äv brothers, —
great wolf-gods. This sack contained the whole
of mankind, and the brothers were bidden to carry
it from the shores of the sea to the Kaibab Plateau,
and by no means to open the package on the way
lest, as with Pandora's box, untold evils should be
turned loose. But, overcome by curiosity, the
younger Cin-au'-äv untied the sack's mouth, when
the majority of people swarmed out. The elder
Cin-au'-äv hastened to close it again and carry it
to the Kaibab Plateau, where those who had remained in the bag found a beautiful home. Those
who had escaped were scattered, and became
Navahos, Mokis, Dakotas, white men, and all the
rest of the outside world — poor sorry fragments
of humanity without the original language of the
gods; and it was all the fault of that careless coyote, Cin-au'-äv.

The quick wits and inquiring mind of the prairie-
wolf serve him not only in chasing, but in saving
himself from being chased. A new enemy has
lately arisen, however, that puts him on his mettle.
This is the practice of chasing him with hounds

after the manner of fox-hunting which is largely pursued now as a sport at army posts in the West, and here and there by townspeople and ranchmen. It began, I think, and has been most diligently developed among the colonists in the interior of British Columbia, where a pack of hounds, recruited largely from the famous Badminton Kennels, in England, has long been maintained at Ashcroft, in the Fraser valley.

The hounds take to this new sport readily, yet the wily and swift-footed wolf is often able to keep out of their way, and save his brush in some rocky retreat, after leading the horsemen a run which sets every nerve a tingling.

Next to the wolverine, the prairie-wolf is, perhaps, the wariest of the animals — not excepting the fox — against which the trapper pits himself. To poisoned meat he falls a victim through his gluttony, and in this way the ranchmen destroy great numbers annually; but he is rarely trapped. The old writer Say tells, with a touch of glee, how his friend Titian Peale, who was a naturalist as well as a painter, was baffled in trying to catch a live coyote for his father's famous Museum — one of the sights of old Philadelphia.

Peale's first experiment was with a " figure-four," and came to nought because a wolf burrowed under the floor and pulled the bait down between the planks. " This procedure," sagely remarks Mr. Say, " would seem to be the result of a faculty

I

beyond mere instinct." A cage was next con-
structed, into which the wolves might enter, but
out of which they could not depart. The coyotes
came, admired the arrangement, sang doleful
lamentations over the bait, which they could see
and smell but could not taste, and went away
again.

Disappointed here, Mr. Peale next began a series
of experiments with steel traps, one of which, pro-
fusely baited, was concealed among the leaves.
Plenty of tracks alone rewarded this effort. "You
can't live on tracks" is one of the aphorisms of
the Plains. Then a seductive bait was suspended
above the trap in the midst of several other pieces;
but the expected victims, stepping circumspectly,
carried off all the meat except the one piece it was
intended they should take. Baits were next hung
up as before, the trap was buried in leaves and
these were burned, so that the trap, scorched free
from any odor of human hands, lay covered with
ashes; still the one bait over the steel jaws was
avoided, and no sinewy foot was pinched. Finally
a wicked arrangement of innocent-looking logs set
on a trigger was made to fall upon the wolf and
destroy him. Peale got his "specimen," but it
was only by brute force: the coyote had been a
match for him in brains.

The remarkable craftiness of this animal, together with its secretive disposition, nocturnal
prowling, and power of annoyance, have caused

the coyote to figure prominently in the myths and religious histories of nearly all the native races of the far west, especially southward; and a collection of these stories from the writings of Powell, Powers, Bandelier, Cushing, Curtin and others would suggest to every reader the Reynard of European folklore, not to speak of other interesting parallels.

The skins of these wolves are not as highly valued as those of the bigger gray wolf, yet formerly they entered largely into the shipments of the Hudson's Bay Company, for whom they were "cased," or stripped off inside out, as is done with smaller fur-bearers, such as the beaver and ermine. At present they are in demand to some extent for making sleigh-robes, rugs, and so forth, and to a less degree for mantles and boas, but can scarcely be accounted among the commercial furs.

The striking resemblance between the coyote and the majority of the snappish curs thronging in the camps of the redskins long ago attracted attention, and with good reason, for these dogs are descended from tamed wolves and foxes of one kind or another, and the stock was, and is yet, constantly replenished by their masters through mixture with the wild wolves.

As a pet the coyote is not in great favor. He will, indeed, stay at home, and will consent to friendly, and even affectionate, terms with his owner, but he seems to have not a particle of gratitude, nor any of that responsive attachment that makes the well-bred dog so lovable as a friend.

Moreover, in spite of his natural subtlety and shrewdness, he shows little aptitude for learning the ordinary accomplishments of dogs, and so fails to sustain an interest in him after the novelty of first acquaintance passes off. Perhaps this seeming inaptitude is really unwillingness, since he may easily regard the things sought to be taught him as beneath his serious attention. If so, the fact that he is occasionally seen as one of the showman's performing animals is all the more noticeable; since unquestionably he could say to the audience, —

"I could show you a trick worth two o' that."

It is a fact, however, that his habits are changing in many particulars with the change in his environment that has been so rapidly brought about in the West; and it will be interesting to observe how far, and in what direction this proceeds in the future.

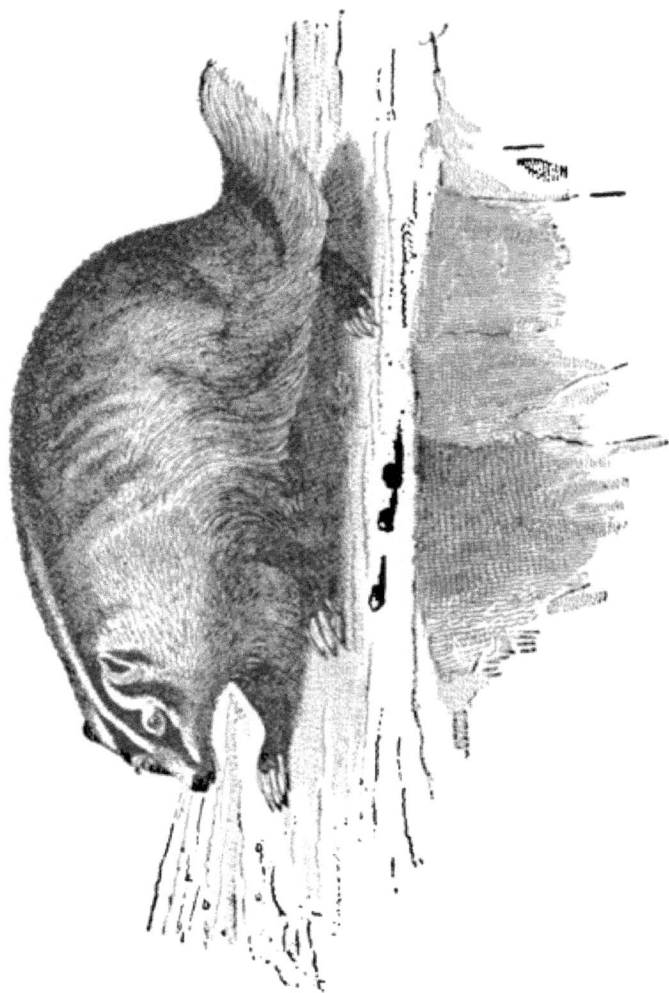

THE AMERICAN BADGER. — After Godman.

V

THE BADGER AND HIS KIN

MANY an animal lives beside us, of which we are told by those genial vagabonds, the hunters, or whose traces constantly present themselves, but of which we rarely catch even a glimpse. These creatures continue to pursue their own secluded manner of living, while men increase around them, and civilization alters their environment, accommodating themselves as well as they can to human interference with their habits and subsistence, and surviving or even profiting by the changes, but keeping aloof from the eyes of men.

I have been using the word "animals" here in its special popular sense of designating the four-footed, hairy creatures technically termed Mammals; and it is a curious and notable lack in our English speech that we have no vernacular word which exactly stands for this most definite and familiar of zoölogical groups: "quadruped" won't do, where precision is desirable, since many reptiles, as lizards and turtles, have four feet; and I see no help for it but to popularize the word "mammal," which is not a very "hard" one to learn.

The birds, or at any rate many of them, seem to welcome the coming of mankind, and to make friends with him at once, and occasionally to follow him into wider countries. Thus the swift, the barn-swallow, and the eave-swallow have abandoned in the east their habits of nesting in hollow trees and upon rocky cliffs or clay-banks, and now make their homes altogether in the chimneys of houses and under the eaves and roofs of barns and outhouses. The phœbe-bird so generally chooses the exposed timbers of bridges that it is more widely known as the bridge-pewee than by any other name ; yet it as often places its adobe cabin on the beam of a shed or porch, as if seeking human company. The grouse, quail, crow, and some other birds have moved westward with the advancing migration of agriculture; and everywhere, no doubt, the total of singing-birds has been greatly increased by the civilizing of the land. Thus we make daily observation of most of the birds, and only need to attend to them more minutely to become aware of the presence of those kinds more rare or occasional.

With the mammals the case is different. Almost the only kinds, not voluntarily domesticated, that have attached themselves to mankind, are the rats and mice — cosmopolitan pests, presumably of Asiatic origin, which have now spread all over the world. Many beasts, as the big game and fiercer carnivores, have almost or quite disappeared

from the more completely civilized regions, for
one reason or another; while others, as the hares
and squirrels, because of their prolificacy and comparative worthlessness, can maintain themselves
everywhere, despite their conspicuous manner
of life.   The muskrat is a singular example of
this faculty, and it has probably augmented rather
than diminished in numbers in the United States
since the civilization of the land, in the face of
steady persecution on account of its value on the
one hand, and, on the other, because it is harmful
to certain human enterprises.

But besides these classes there is a group of
mammals, fellow-denizens with us of the cultivated
parts of the country, that persist, and in some
cases increase, yet escape the notice of all but a
few persons, and continue to live their own lives
regardless of us and our operations.

What do the most of us see or know, for example, of the wild mice, half a dozen species of
which are numerous everywhere in our woods and
fields? Yet thousands of these small and active
creatures, — the lovely red and white deer or
vesper mouse (Hesperomys), the various short-
tailed brown meadow-mice (Arvicolæ), the far-
leaping, kangaroo-like jumping-mouse (Zapus),
and several others allied to them, — inhabit all
our forests, prairies, fields, and gardens.   They
are beyond counting, and form the principal game
of a large number of wild animals, — mammals,

birds, and reptiles, without whose assistance we should be unable to endure their hordes, — while the results of their pernicious activity are constantly apparent. Read this extract from Kennicott's masterly but nearly forgotten papers on the mammals of Illinois, and note how important a factor in the relations of men and animals are these unseen foes : he is speaking more particularly of the true meadow-mice of the genus *Arvicola*, but we may take his statements as good for the whole class.

"The food and general habits of the different species are much alike, though some prefer high, and others wet ground ; while others inhabit the woods, prairies, etc. All the species burrow, and none climb trees. The common food of those I have observed is the grasses and other herbaceous plants, their seeds and roots, and the seeds and acorns, as well as the bark, of trees in the woods, with grain and vegetables, when inhabiting cultivated fields. Some are omnivorous, as has been observed in their habits while in captivity. To what extent they eat animal food when at liberty, I am unable to say, though it is probable that they consume some insects in summer ; and they may even obtain a few, with the pupæ and eggs of more, concealed in the grass traversed by them in winter. Some kinds, at least, lay up stores of food for winter. All are active at this time, moving about in the coldest weather, and never hibernate like marmots.

"One characteristic, certainly possessed by all the species in common, is their ability to destroy the products of the farm. I know of no mammals more injurious to the farmers in northern Illinois than these seemingly insignificant meadow-mice. Few, if any, escape their depredations, though the full amount of damage done by them is but little known; and yet they are usually thought unworthy of consideration. Such of our farmers as cut their corn and leave it standing for some time in the field, as is usually done here, will find, upon examination, that in many, if not every one, of the shocks there may be found one or more pair of meadow-mice, which have dug for themselves burrows in the ground beneath, and have carried thither a store of corn; while in these, or ensconced in the protecting corn-stalks above, they have built themselves a nest, in which they can lead a very comfortable sort of life, regaling themselves, when hungry, upon the corn. Now a pair of mice will not, it is true, eat enough corn to alarm a farmer for the safety of his crop; but let any one examine a large field of corn, thus cut and left standing on the ground a month or two, where these mice abound, and carefully estimate the amount of corn destroyed in each shock, observing that which has been buried in the burrow, and then multiply that by the number of shocks inhabited by these pests, and it will often be found that they have really consumed or destroyed a large amount. In meadows they do much injury by devouring the roots and stems of Timothy, clover, and other plants used for hay. This mischief, however, is seldom noticed by farmers; or, if it is at all, in districts where moles abound, all the blame is laid upon them, as, indeed, is very much of the damage done by meadow-mice wherever the two exist together. They also do great mischief by killing young plants in grain-fields; and, soon after the seed is sown, they destroy many of the grains, little stores of which may be found collected in shallow excavations. These are often not eaten, and, germinating, astonish and scandalize the farmer by the appearance of a thick clump of plants where he thought he had sown his seed quite uniformly. They also dig up grain that has just sprouted; and, by examining fields of young wheat, oats, etc., spots will be seen where they have dug down, guided by the growing blades, and taken off the grain. In a nursery, where apple-seeds were planted in autumn, I have observed that, during fall and spring, so many of the seeds were dug up by these mice as to leave long gaps in the rows of seedlings, the empty shells of the seeds being found lying about the rows from which they had been taken. They congregate in stacks of grain and hay, — sometimes in exceedingly great numbers, — destroying all the lower parts by cutting galleries through them in every direction.

"The greatest mischief done by meadow-mice is the gnawing of bark from fruit-trees. The complaints are constant and grievous throughout the Northern States of the destruction of orchard and nursery trees by the various species of arvicolæ. The entire damage done by them in this way may be estimated, perhaps, at millions of dollars. . . . This is especially the case at the West, where no care is taken to protect the trees against them, — careless orchardists allowing grass to grow about the roots of their fruit-trees, and

Blarina brevicauda

Sorex cooperi

Sorex vagrans

Urotrichus gibbsi

thus kindly furnishing the arvicolæ with excellent nesting-places in winter, and rendering the trees doubly liable to be girdled. In the nurseries in northern Illinois, I have seen whole rows of young apple-trees stripped of their bark for a foot or two above the ground. Thousands of fruit-trees, as well as evergreens and other ornamental trees and shrubs, are at times thus killed in a nursery in one winter. . . . Many times in spring, when a florist uncovers some choice plant he has carefully protected during the winter by straw, etc., he is grieved and chagrined to find, instead of a fine Dianthus, or half-hardy rose, two nimble, black-eyed arvicolæ, which have found good winter quarters in the shelter provided for the plant that has furnished them food. No little injury do they to vegetables of all kinds, destroying the young plants of peas, beans, cabbages, etc., as well as digging up seeds of all sorts, and gnawing potatoes, beets, and other roots."

How often do we see these creatures, so numerous and ubiquitous? How unexpected would be an accidental discovery of their presence, were it not for their too familiar assaults upon our grain-fields, granaries, and gardens? And how clever they are in their mischief!

Then there are the shrews.[1] Two or three kinds of these tiniest of quadrupeds, looking like miniature mice, until you examine them, — note

[1] See Plate of Shrews, opposite: *Blarina brevicauda*, — common short-tailed shrew of the eastern United States. *Sorex cooperi*, — an eastern long-tailed shrew; the smallest of known mammals. *Sorex vagrans*, — a common Western long-tailed shrew. *Urotrichus gibbsi*, — the curious shrew-mole of the Pacific coast,

the prolonged flexible snout and delicate rows of
needle-pointed teeth, made to seize, hold, and
crush the hard, slippery bodies of insects, — inhabit
by thousands every part of the country, and are
active at all seasons of the year; yet only now and
then is one seen, and that one is usually dead.
Mainly nocturnal in their work, and sneaking from
point to point under leaves and through runways
concealed by the arching grasses, they elude our
notice while existing in multitudes about our feet.

Of the moles we seem to know somewhat more,
for the heaved-up lines of turf that mark their subterranean lines of research for bugs and worms,
and the hillocks of loose earth, showing where, at
intervals, they have cast out the excavated soil,
are familiar to all dwellers outside of large cities.
Nevertheless, so infrequently is the miner himself
met with, that many a person who has grumbled
all his life at the depredations on his lawn, would
not recognize the culprit when brought before
him, and certainly could not tell whether it were
the common garden-mole, or the star-nosed one,
or Brewer's hairy-tailed mole.[1]   These animals, it

---

[1] See Plate of Common Moles, opposite : 1. The eastern Garden-
Mole (*Scalops aquaticus*); *a*, head, side view; *b*, palm of fore-foot;
c, semi-naked tail. 2. The Star-nosed Mole (*Condylura cristata*);
a, head, under side; *b*, palm; *c*, tail; *d*, "star" of the muzzle,
front view. 3. The California Shrew-mole (*Urotrichus gibbsi*);
a, head, under side; *b*, head, side view (see also Plate of Shrews;
c, palm. 4. The Hairy-tailed, or Brewer's Mole (*Scapanus
breweri*); *a*, muzzle, side view; *b*, tail; *c*, palm.

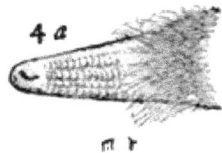

4 a

m r

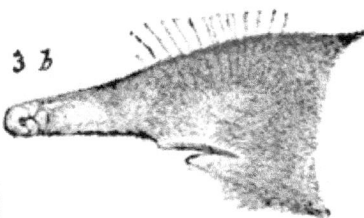

3 b

4 b

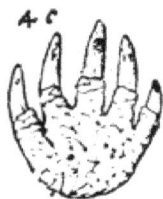

4 c

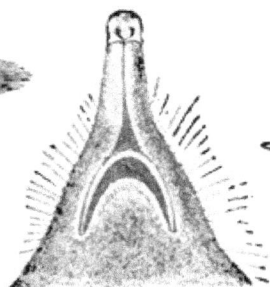

3. a

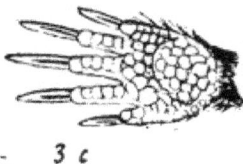

3 c

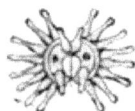

2 d

5

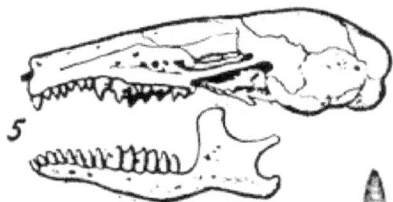

2.a

2 b

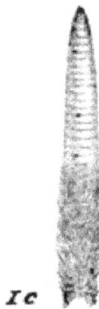

1c

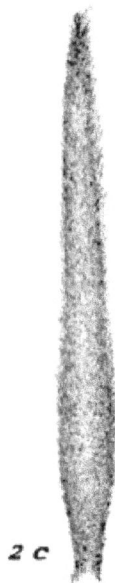

2 c

1. b

K

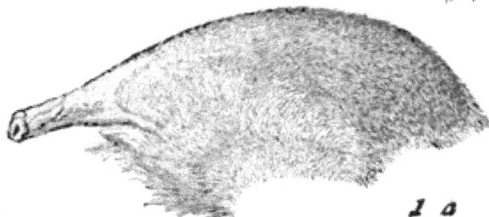

1 a

129

is true, are mainly nocturnal, but they often come to the surface and wander about, even on the snow, as also do the shrews. These open-air excursions are made usually in the dusk of early dawn and late evening, or during rains; but they also have the curious custom of coming out for a saunter precisely at noon, so that it is surprising that they are not more often seen.

The moles are blind, having only rudimentary eyes, but their ears and sense of touch are extremely acute, enabling them to detect not only the sound, but the jar of approaching footsteps, and hasten into their shelters. The mole is frequently revealed to us for the first time by finding one lying dead on the turf. There will be no sign of violence about its body, nor of disease; and it is lying out on the grass in the daylight, careless of the exposure that all its life long had been its dread. What killed it? Does it feel death approaching and creep out of its cellar to end its days under the blue sky and in the sweet air? Do the other moles, foreseeing its fate, drive it forth? I have no answer; but the explanation is probably far more prosaic than that. Shrews, closely allied to the moles, and among the hardiest of animals, dwelling upon almost arctic mountain tops, and braving the severest winter weather, often perish in an equally mysterious manner. I have more than once had one die in a short time after capture, although it had not been hurt in the slightest degree, and everything had been done to make it comfortable. Was this death due to nervous alarm? There seems no other explanation of it.

The deer, wild-cat, bear, raccoon, mink, weasel, skunk, muskrat, porcupine, beaver (but how rare is the sight of a living beaver, even after one has found its tenanted dams!) and the great company of squirrels, gophers, and the like, we know pretty well, and feel their presence in our woods, waters, and prairies; but who has seen, or ever hopes to see, an otter, although these fine animals still secrete themselves in all parts of the Union? Thoreau relates that when he spoke of this animal to the oldest doctor in Concord, who should be, he thought, *ex officio*, a naturalist, the worthy physician was greatly surprised at the suggestion that it lived in Massachusetts, although he recalled that the Pilgrims sent home a great number of otter skins, among other peltries, in the first ship that returned to England. Then Thoreau proceeded to inform him of what he had seen that day, — the 6th of December, 1856, at 2 P.M., as recorded in his diary :

"To Hubbard's Bridge and Holden Swamp, and up river on ice. . . . Just this side of Bittern Cliff, I see the very remarkable track of an otter, made undoubtedly December 3d, when the snow-ice was mere slush. It had come up through a hole (now black ice) by the stem of a button-bush, and apparently pushed its way through the slush, as through snow on land, leaving a track eight inches wide, more or less, with the now frozen snow shoved up two inches above the general level on each side. . . . I saw where these creatures had been playing, sliding or fishing, apparently to-day, on the snow-covered rocks, on which for a rod upwards, and as much in width, the snow was trodden and worn quite smooth, as if twenty had trodden and slid there for several hours. Their droppings are a mass of fishes' scales and bones, loose, scaly, black masses. . . . The river was all tracked up with otters from Bittern Cliff upward. Sometimes one had trailed his tail edgewise, making a mark like the tail of a deer-mouse; sometimes they were moving fast, and there was an interval of five feet between the tracks. . . . These very conspicuous tracks generally commenced and terminated at some button-bush or willow where black ice now marked the hole of that date. . . . In many places the otters appeared to have gone floundering along in the slushy ice and water."

But even Thoreau did not see the animal itself, then nor at any other time, though once one crawled past the door of his Walden house in the night and set him a-thinking — but it didn't need a noble otter to do that!

Dr. Charles Abbott saw them several times, twenty or thirty years ago, in the Delaware and its tributaries near Trenton; Merriam mentions

encountering three at once in the Adirondacks, and
Audubon and Bachman had one or two personal in-
terviews in the South; but these were naturalists and
trappers who made it their business to seek and
find the sly creature in its haunts, yet succeeded
rather by perseverance and good luck than by
foresight.   Many have tried equally hard, perhaps,
and have failed.

I know where one lives, in a little river not far
from the city of New York; but I shall by no
means tell you the river's name, for he must not
be disturbed.   It is a great pleasure to me to think
that this stream, which for a large part of its
course flows between cultivated fields, is spanned
by highways and bound like Ixion to the miller's
wheel, still harbors an animal so truly wild and
aboriginal.   It is a picturesque and poetic relic of
the prehistoric wilderness, and a romantic reminder
of the free, primitive, savage state of things, as
refreshing to the imagination as the pungent odor
of spruce-leaves in a winter drawing-room.

A more remarkable example, perhaps, of an
animal that secretes itself well from observation
while numerous throughout its range is found in
the badger.   Although it is comparatively large,
predatory, and common, it spends most of its time
underground, rarely comes abroad except during
the hours of darkness, and makes haste to hide
itself the moment it detects the approach of any
human being.   The sight of a living badger is

therefore an uncommon accident, even where the species abounds and its burrows may be seen in all directions; and the animal disappears rapidly before the advance of any considerable settlement in its territory. Audubon and Bachman imply that its habitat was always limited by the eastern extent of the Great Plains, but the fact is that these animals formerly were spread as far east as the open country extended, dwelling upon all the prairies of southwestern Michigan, northern Ohio, Indiana, Illinois, Wisconsin (which has been called the Badger State since its early days), Minnesota, Iowa, and northward. Now they have disappeared from all this area, and are rare in the easterly and more cultivated districts of Kansas, Nebraska, and Dakota, where their range is annually withdrawing westward. Northward they are found as far as the Peace River, and eastward to Hudson Bay; so that the fullest early accounts of them were given in the writings of Pennant, Richardson, and other naturalists who explored the Fur Countries years ago.

Everywhere the badger is truly a "beast of the fields" — an inhabitant of the open country — digging or stealing underground holes, and preying upon everything it can catch or conquer. Its body is two feet long, extraordinarily low-hung and broad, so that the creature appears to be, and perhaps is, wider than it is tall; but this effect is partly due to the fact that the long fur, which parts upon the spine as if carefully brushed toward each flank, is loose and flaring at the sides, giving the animal the appearance of having a rather stiff fur blanket balanced across its back. The legs are short and firm, and the large feet are furnished with long and very strong claws, making them powerful digging-tools. The tail is short and thick. The head is broad, massive, and dog-like, with round, furry ears, a hairy muzzle, and jaws filled with formidable teeth, scarcely less terrible than those of the wolverine. The whole squat, compact, large-boned, massively skulled form indicates great muscular power ; and it is controlled by a capable brain and an indomitable spirit.

"As gray as a badger" is a proverbial expression that originated, probably, almost in the beginnings of speech, and in reference to the European badger, which has much the same general appearance and methods as ours, but anatomically is somewhat different. The loose fur is a "grizzle of blackish, with white, gray, or tawny," each hair having all these colors on some part of its length, and the whole blending handsomely. The colors vary greatly, however, with season, age, and health, and in the high, arid interior of the country are always much lighter, less tawny, than in the moister, easier climate of the Pacific Slope. The fur of the under side of the body is more uniformly whitish than on the upper parts, except as to the feet, which are blackish brown. The head is strikingly marked, the general color, from the back of the neck forward, being dark brown, broken by a distinct white stripe from the bridge of the nose back to the nape of the neck, and a somewhat irregular white stripe on each cheek, reaching from the corners of the mouth to near the top of the ears; below this, on each side, is a crescentic, dark-colored patch, separating the stripes from the white of the ears and throat. These conspicuous markings give to the countenance an expression of native ability and shrewdness in the disguise of a painted clown; and they set one a-thinking.

Belonging to the great family of "fur-bearing" carnivores, the Mustelidæ, which begins with the weasels and ends with the sea-otters, and is related to the bears on one side and to the dogs on the other, the badgers occupy a midway place in their own group, between the skunks and otters, and form the subfamily Melinæ. Species of this subfamily inhabit Europe, Asia, and America, but those of the Old World are of different genera from ours. Thus, the common badger of Europe, well known in Great Britain and elsewhere, is *Meles vulgaris*, and allied species belong to most parts of Asia; their habits are much like those of the American forms. The small, fetid, burrowing teledu, or stinking badger of the mountains of Java and Sumatra, is *Mydaus meliceps*. The sand-badger, a large pig-like species of the mountains

of northeastern India and Assam, is *Arctonyx
collaris*, having near relatives in the farther East.
By recent authors the skunks, the honey-badgers,
(Mellivora), the Cape of Good Hope polecats
(Ictonyx), and the small Oriental burrowers of the
genus Helictis, are also put into this section.   Our
American species have a genus of their own named
Taxidea, of which there are two species, *Taxidea
americana*, our common Northern form, and the
Mexican badger, tejon or tlacoyote (*T. berlandieri*),
but the latter is probably only a geographical variety
of the former.   Everywhere these animals agree
in having long fur, without much ornament, in
their choice of open, somewhat elevated habitats,
in exhibiting courage and voracity, in nocturnal
disposition, in making their homes in burrows, and
in possessing perineal glands secreting a fetid
liquor, which in some species, and especially at
the breeding season, makes them extremely offensive to human nostrils.

So much for the badger's place in nature.

In regard to the habits of our American badger
not much is to be said, due both to the fact that
the animal is so secretive that we have small opportunity to study it, and to the further circum-
stance that its life is exceedingly simple.   In such
favorable regions as the dry plains that stretch
from the Rio Grande to the North Saskatchewan,
the animal is still numerous.   Besides the countless
herds of buffaloes, antelopes, and the lesser, but

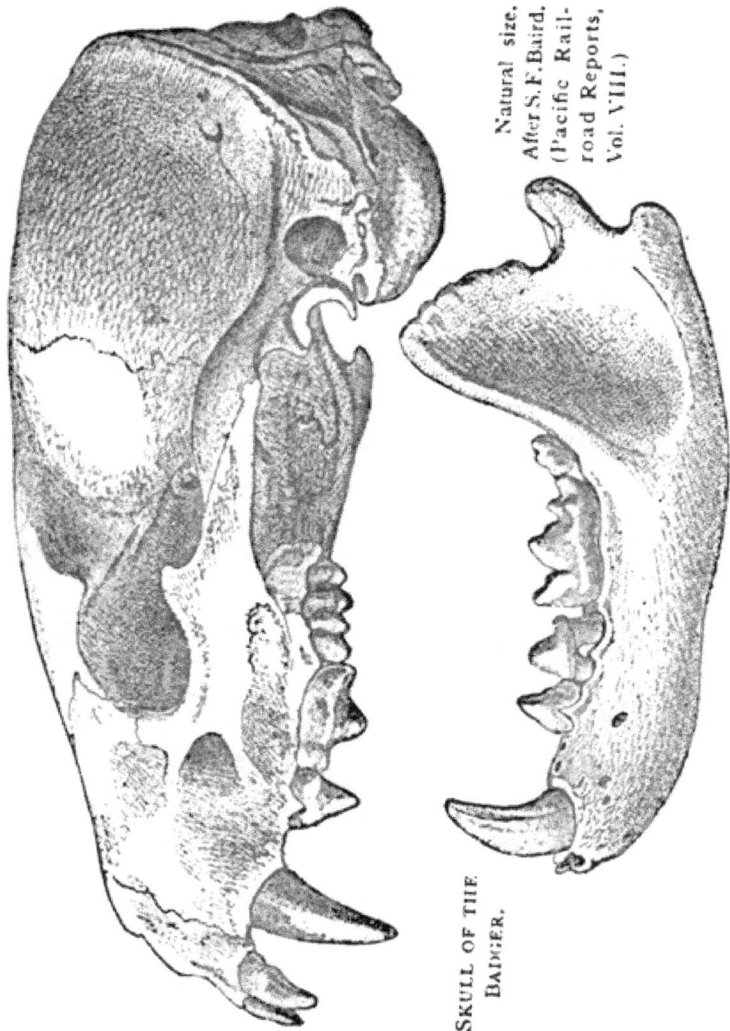

SKULL OF THE BADGER.

Natural size.
After S. F. Baird.
(Pacific Rail-
road Reports,
Vol. VIII.)

still numerous, bands of deer that originally roamed
over them, and gave sustenance to a much larger
population of Indians than we are now accustomed
to remember, these vast pastures teemed with small
creatures.   Everywhere, in spite of their early reputation as a desert, the plains were clothed with
vegetation, and this harbored hordes of insects.
Thousands of square miles of grasses, forage
plants, and low, fruit-bearing shrubs not only furnished almost unlimited pasture for the bison,
antelope, and deer, but also gave, in the way of
stems, leaves, seeds, and fruits, food for an innumerable population of small animals able to
exist without a great amount of water.   Thus the
plains abounded in a large variety of seed-eating,
ground-haunting birds, together with many insect-
catching and predatory kinds; in snakes of many
species and certain other land reptiles; and in a
long list of rodents — ground-squirrels, gophers,
and the like; while even some aquatic and arboreal
animals followed the larger rivers far into the
plains country.

Such an aggregation of peaceful animal life,
whose unfortunate part it seems to be, in the
inscrutable ordering of the world, to furnish food
for the other, fiercer, half of the denizens of the
globe, would of course attract an army of flesh-
eating creatures, eager to prey upon their weaker
brethren, and able to struggle with one another
for the spoils of rapine and robbery.   After the

big grazers — the buffaloes, deer, antelope and, later, the wild horses — came the bears, the puma, the jaguar, wild-cats, and wolves, none of which despised more humble prey in moments of hunger; while the birds, reptiles, and lesser mammals were incessantly pursued by a host of smaller birds and beasts of prey, among which our badger took a prominent rank.

The existence of all these — marauder and marauded — depended, and still depends, upon their ability to cope with a climate which adds to its cardinal disadvantage of great aridity the characteristic of going to great extremes of both heat and cold. These details may seem wide of our subject, but it is highly interesting to note the kind of country in which our "hero" chooses to dwell, and also who are his companions, and the means by which they maintain themselves in the competition of life. Now, whatever may be their relations with each other, the year's weather — the climate — is a fact that all have to reckon with alike.

The dry summer heats are not very prejudicial to the birds, and when pasturage has been parched out in one locality the grazing quadrupeds can move to another; therefore these are able to avoid the rigors and famine of winter by fleeing to a gentler Southern region, as all such animals do, according to their various necessities, followed by the big cats and wolves. But with all the smaller animals, from the badger down to the mouse and lizard, who cannot migrate, it becomes a case, literally, of " Root, hog, or die!" Shelter must be had, and as the only shelter possible is beneath the ground, every creature that cannot get away in the fall digs a hole in which to pass the winter. When human pioneers decide to brave a winter on the plains they do substantially the same thing, and for the same reason ; for an Oklahoma " dugout" is scarcely more than a burrow, furnished with skins and cloth instead of grass and leaves ; and both boomers and gophers find these homes beneath the sod highly serviceable against the heats and dust-storms of summer, as well as against the blasts and snows of winter.

In plainer language, then, no resident mammals, with a few rare and partial exceptions, can make their homes upon the open plains of our West, or on the pampas of South America, on the Karoo of southern or the Sahara of northern Africa, or the steppes of Russia or Central Asia, unless they have acquired the knowledge and power of burrowing. It is probable that in all stages of the globe's development, since land animals began to roam upon it, at least, there have been wide areas devoid of forest, and these were no doubt inhabited from the beginning, inasmuch as some of the earliest mammalian forms of which we have any traces seem by their structure to have been adapted to this manner of life. It is, moreover, almost wholly among the plains-dwelling, burrow-making animals that the phenomenon of hibernation is observed, and a reason for this coincidence will be apparent to any one who gives the subject a few moments' thought.

A burrow, however, affords safety against their enemies to only a few of the largest and strongest of the animals habitually digging or using it, of which our badger is himself, perhaps, the best example. With him, his house is a castle. He is a rapid and powerful digger, and seems to make more holes than he has use for. Audubon and Bachman describe the work done in this direction by one they had in captivity, as follows:

"He would fall to work with his strong feet and long nails, and in a minute bury himself in the earth, and would very soon advance to the end of a chain ten feet in length. In digging, the hind as well as the fore feet were at work, the latter for the purpose of excavating, and the former (like paddles) for expelling the earth out of the hole, and nothing seemed to delight him more than burrowing in the ground; he never seemed to become weary of this kind of amusement; and when he had advanced to the length of his chain he would return and commence a fresh gallery near the mouth of the first hole; thus he would be occupied for hours, and it was necessary to drag him away by main force."

It is noticeable, in view of the above, that the

captive mentioned hereafter seemed to know nothing about tunnelling — had had no chance to learn the art, in fact!

This animal is firm on its feet, very strong, armed with formidable teeth, and is an indomitable fighter. It was accounted high in the list of beasts giving "greate dysporte" according to the ancient canons of venery; and badger-baiting, once a popular recreation among our British forefathers, has not yet been wholly abandoned by the ruder of their descendants. In early times it was customary to place the captive destined to furnish the amusement near a hole dug in the ground for his refuge, and then to send the dogs at him singly. The favorite sort for this work was a long-bodied, long-jawed hound, which, as the badger was then frequently called the "grey," came to be known as a "greyhound." Nowadays, when the sport is attempted, a barrel is furnished instead of the snugger hole in the ground, and a number of dogs are set upon the poor beast at once — an example of how such cruel sports naturally descend into mere torture. This villanous practice will soon entirely disappear, but its memory will be perpetuated in the expressive verb, "to badger."

While, then, he can and does put up a good fight if attacked when abroad, he never fails to make strenuous efforts to gain the strategic position afforded by the mouth of his tunnel, — the sallyport of his fortress, — where he makes a

L

stand against anything no bigger than a wolf, at least, without hesitation. But such encounters are no doubt rare, for he seems to have no enemy; that is, no beast, so far as I know, habitually preys upon or wars against him, though he must quarrel with a savage rival, now and then, and occasionally have to exert himself to overcome resistance by his victims. The only creature he has much reason to dread is the rattlesnake, and he probably knows how to manage him, not to speak of the considerable protection his long coat and loose hide afford against harm from the serpent's fangs. The animal's strength is remarkable, measured otherwise than by its fossorial feats. Lying flat on its back, it rises with ease to a sitting posture, unaided by its fore paws. A captive one, less than two years old, would shove aside a loaded Saratoga trunk that it required two men to handle, and once moved a heavy kitchen range from the corner to the middle of the room.

The badger feeds upon whatever animal food he can kill or catch that is not carrion. He may pounce upon a slow-moving snake, toad, or lizard; may creep up to the hare in its form, or to a bird upon its nest, and if he fail in the latter case, for he is not very spry, will console himself with a mess of eggs; even insects are acceptable, and captives take almost anything that is offered them, usually sitting up and holding the morsel in their paws like a squirrel.

His principal food, nevertheless, consists of the ground-squirrels, gophers, and field-mice among which he lives. It is beyond his ability to chase and catch these nimble fellows, for the badger is slow and clumsy; but it "is the work of a very few minutes for this vigorous miner to so far enlarge their burrows that it can reach the deepest recesses."

Right here an interesting point may be considered. Where the prairie-dogs and other spermophiles are especially numerous (and they exist in countless thousands in certain districts of the Great Plains, Columbia Basin, and southern California), there badgers gather in corresponding numbers, attracted by the abundance of food; and they must often encounter one another, as well as the coyote, kit-fox, ferret, and other raiders, bound upon the same bloody quest. To this contingency the curious pattern of coloring on the badger's face seems to bear direct reference, if the speculations of the natural-selectionists have any basis in fact; but I am not aware that this point has been mentioned by Poulton or other exponents of the philosophy of animal coloration. Let us examine it.

The only part of a badger visible when it is sitting in the mouth of its burrow, as it likes to do, or is threading its way through some underground passage, must be its face. Now this is the only part of the animal that bears any distinctive color-mark, the remainder of the body being simply

an indeterminate gray. The sharply contrasted
stripes of white and dark brown upon its countenance would be visible when anything could be
seen at all, and would instantly apprise any creature what kind of visitor was approaching. These
stripes, then, are really excellent examples of what
Mr. A. R. Wallace calls "recognition colors," and
frequently also of "warning colors." Man or brute
catching a glimpse, in the shadow of a hole, of this
clownish visage, as impersonal as the bodiless grin
of the Cheshire Cat that astonished Alice in Won-
derland, would know at once that a badger's form
and ferocity were behind it, and would act accord-
ingly. An exact parallel is found in the blackfooted ferret, whose dwelling-place and methods
of underground foray are similar to those of our
subject, and which is conspicuously marked only
on the face. In neither case would awkward mis-
takes arise when friends or allies met in the corri-
dors of their own or an enemy's castle, for their
very foreheads would bear the family crest. The
badger's name itself is a curious historical affirma-
tion of this scientific proposition. It means simply
the wearer of a badge, — the marked animal. The
old French *blaireau*, still current among the
French-Canadians of the far Northwest (in the
corrupt form "braro"), had an identical signifi-
cance; and apparently the same is true of the
early English term *brock*, — probably of Celtic
origin, — which survives to this day in the north-

ern dialects of Great Britain. This last is the con-
temptuous epithet that Shakespeare employs in
"Twelfth Night" (Act 2, Scene 5) when he makes
Sir Toby Belch mutter an aside of annoyance over
Malvolio's reading of the dropped letter, — "Marry,
hang thee, Brock!" And do you not remember the
curious part of "next friend," or counsel and go-
between, that Grimbart, the badger, plays in the
legend of Reynard, the Fox?

It is amazing to see, in such favorable tracts as
have been mentioned, how the ground is pitted
and honey-combed with old and new burrows of
all sorts. The danger of your horse stepping into
an open hole is doubled by the chance of his crush-
ing through the roofs of unsuspected excavations.
Cattle-herding horses must acquire dexterity in
avoiding such accidents, or they would break their
limbs and risk their riders' necks fifty times a day.
I shall never forget a wild morning I once spent
near Cheyenne, hunting antelopes with deerhounds.
The prairie horses — mine was a nervous gray that
seemed unable to stand on all four legs at once —
were eager to enter into the fun, and bore us
straight across the country, up the ridges and
down the hollows, over or around the clumps of
sage and grease-wood, at topmost speed, twisting
and dodging to avoid badger-earths, ant-hillocks,
prairie-dog holes, and tall bushes; and more than
once my horse seemed to take a new flight in the
air, when he rose to leap over a thicket, and caught

sight of an unexpected hole on the other side. I managed to stay with him wherever he went, and came back all right; yet it is a marvel that none of us lost our seats, if not our lives, in that wild chase. But we caught the antelope!

The entrance to the burrow of a badger is much larger than that to a prairie-dog's hole, and no hillock is raised about it. It reaches below the frost-line, and may be almost any length. The animal changes its abode frequently, and constantly digs more holes than it needs, thereby saving a great deal of labor for coyotes, foxes, ferrets, etc., who take possession of its abandoned entrenchments and probably are welcome to them. They form a retreat for snakes, too, Dr. Suckley making the gruesome note that in western Minnesota, about 1857, he found old badger-earths inhabited by vast numbers of a gregarious species of garter-snake: " I have seen at times, at the bottom of a vacated hole, a dozen or more in a knot — the writhing, excessively serpentine mass disgusting all but the naturalist." The rattlesnake is a frequent and dangerous tenant in the Southwest; and the prairie-owl a comical one.

This ubiquitous turning up of the soil, by which, within a century or less, over the widest districts, every square yard of earth, to the depth of several feet, must be brought to the surface, and exposed to the air, while an enormous amount of fertilizing material has, meanwhile, been dragged into the holes, and there ultimately mingled with the earth, is a most important natural process of soil-preparation, equivalent to the farmer's ploughing and manuring. To the influence that fossorial animals have thus exerted must be largely attributed the decomposition of the surface-rock over an extensive area of the plains, and its change into good soil, highly fertile wherever water is obtainable in suitable quantity. The spread, growth, and decay of plants would accomplish much, and is, perhaps, the chief agency in the production and enrichment of earth; but crumbling rock-sand would be very slowly enriched by such a plant-growth as the short, dry, and sparse herbage of the plains affords, were it not continually exposed to the chemistry of the air, mixed with vegetable and animal manure, and pulverized, by these precursors of agriculture.

Little is known of the reproduction of the badger. Godman tells us that three or four young are born in summer, and that the period of life may reach fifteen years. In the United States the animal is more or less active all winter, being able to search out or dig out enough sleeping ground-squirrels, marmots, etc., in spite of the frost, to satisfy its needs if not its appetite. Farther north, however, the greater cold and enforced famine induce or compel it to pass in semi-torpidity the more severe months of winter.

Year by year the range of this animal is narrowed and its numbers are decreased through the encroachments and persecution of mankind. The Indians kill it for food when they can, but few white men have been able to stomach the flesh, which is tainted to the fancy, if not actually to the palate, with the musky odor that belongs to the animal, and arises from the possession of anal glands, similar to those that make the skunks and many other mustelines odious to us; but our American badger is far less offensive in this respect than are the "stinking" species of the Old World. The fur is prized by the Indians for various special purposes, and enters largely into modern trade, being well adapted and beautiful for robes, overcoats, and the like. The animals, consequently, are trapped and poisoned extensively for the sake of their pelts; while the farmers, with a sadly mistaken sense of propriety, poison and drown them out as nuisances. I say mistaken, because the only harm badgers do, is by digging here and there; while they serve the farmer beneficently by killing off the gophers, rabbits, and ground-squirrels, which, unless their multiplication is restrained, may speedily become a serious pest, as has been shown in California and Kansas. Since badger-baiting has gone out of fashion, and as the animal is not in demand as a pet, efforts are rarely made to take one alive by smoking it out as used to be done. It is a waste of time to try to dig one out, for it can go deeper and deeper as fast as you can follow it.

The following extracts from an account of a tame badger printed by the *Youth's Companion*, in 1896, contain interesting facts. He had not yet opened his eyes when captured, and was brought up on a nursing-bottle. He thrived, and soon became a mischievous pet, constantly under foot. His voice was that of a very young crying baby, but much more noisy; and in extreme anger he would squeal like a pig. When a terrier, whom he was constantly teasing, turned on him, he would tuck his head between his feet and roll himself into a compact furry ball with which the dog could do nothing; but he had not the patience to maintain this attitude of defence very long. He ran almost as well backward as forward, but liked better to reach his destination by rolling over and over instead of walking. As he grew larger, a favorite trick was to open the door of the stove and rake out coals and ashes upon the floor. Although quick to resent any harm (and the grandmother was the only one of the family that dared punish him — before her he was meek), he seemed never to bear resentment or be treacherous, and was well disposed toward strangers. He became fond of chasing the chickens, and would make havoc among the poultry unless prevented.

"Badge," his master records, "is a model housekeeper in his way. He is very fond of cherries, nibbling the food daintily and rejecting the pit. When he has finished eating the cherries he carefully carries the pits to a knothole in the floor of the porch and drops them through it to the ground.

" Every morning when he gets up he carries his bed out of his little house, shakes it thoroughly, and throws it over the boards that fence him in. At night he always carries it back, but through the day it gets thoroughly aired.

" He will beg and scold vociferously if he is not given his daily bath. This he takes in a large dripping-pan, washing first his face and paws, then getting in, first on his belly, then turning on his back. When a mere baby, he fell into a tub of water, which gave him such a scare that any large amount of water will still frighten him ; but he enjoys his shallow pan immensely. His bath fin-ished, he will, unless watched, overturn the pan, taking one edge in his fore feet, which he uses as cleverly as does a bear or a monkey, lifting it up and flopping it over."

These facts are truly interesting, but really they do not throw much light upon the natural habits of the species, for this little representative never had the example or instruction of any of its kind, and, in a thoroughly unbadger-like environment, behaved himself much as any other household pet might do. One would not expect to learn much of the manners and customs of the Eskimos, for instance, from the behavior of a person of that race who had grown up from infancy in New York.

VI

ANIMAL TRAINING AND ANIMAL INTELLIGENCE

IT is a long time since naturalists and philosophers maintained the doctrine that animals were mere machines controlled by an inflexible and impulsive something vaguely called "instinct." All reflective men now believe that the mind of an animal differs from the human intellect only in degree, and to say that brutes have no capability of comprehending new ideas, of acquiring and memorizing novel information, and therefore of improving their minds, would be to go counter to all human experience.

The extent of this capability, however, remains a question, and one upon which close observation of our domestic animals, our pets, and particularly of those animals trained for the amusement of the public, is calculated to throw much light. The study of wild animals in their native haunts may inform us what progress each has made in adapting itself to the natural conditions of its life ; but the study of tamed animals, placed under new conditions and influences, will show whether these are capable of further or, at any rate, divergent advancement intellectually, and give some hint of the probable limits of this progress.

It should be noted that *taming* and *training* are not identical terms. Taming is merely inducing an animal to abandon its natural feral disposition so far as to come under human control and be more or less sociable with man. It is a matter in respect to which animals vary widely, not only as between classes, but as between individuals of the same species. Moreover, tamability seems a matter of disposition rather than of intellect, and perhaps pertains to a lower rather than a higher grade of intelligence, for it is noticeable that some of the animals most clever in the school of the menagerie abandon only slightly, if at all, their native savagery. On the other hand, some animals thoroughly domesticated seem incapable of any considerable degree of education — though perhaps nobody has ever tried it in any proper and continuous way. It would be hazardous to allege that any animal organism is too low to manifest, have we eyes to perceive it, some intelligence superior to simple sensitiveness or unreasoning instinct. It is beyond my purpose, however, to deal here with these almost imperceptible beginnings of brute mind, or indeed with natural intellect in animals at all, but, rather, to hasten on to a view of the acquired knowledge and abilities of the higher, vertebrated animals.

Much might be said in respect to the inferior

orders of these, such as fishes, amphibians, and
reptiles. Examples of all these have been made
pets, and taught some very simple actions; but
the so-called performing serpents of the circus
are not so really, simply submitting to be put
through certain motions in the hands of their
keepers. The South American anaconda seems
to be more amenable than any other snake to instruction, really amounting in some cases to a
trained obedience.

Birds open to view a much wider range of mental capability. Sportsmen need not be reminded
by me of the accurate way in which hawks are
trained by falconers, and cormorants are employed
to bring in fish. Here the natural habits of the
birds are controlled at man's behest; but the education of some small birds has led them far beyond the range of their natural exertions and
aptitudes. Such are the performances of canary
birds and other trained finches, which equal, in
the mental adaptiveness and grasp implied, those
of most of the four-footed performers of the menagerie. These birds will tumble like gymnasts, will
draw tiny carriages, discharge firearms at one
another, drop down in pretence of death, and do
many other diverting feats. They will even sub-
mit to be handled by the clown's dogs and cats,
showing no fear of these, their ancient ogres.

Though finches are usually selected for this
kind of training, there seems no reason why a

variety of other birds would not be as amenable
to the patient zeal of their educators. A long list
of birds have been made pets of, but none more
prettily than the clouds of doves which wheel
about the head of an *équestrienne* as she gallops
swiftly about the ring of a circus, displaying her
supple body in graceful attitudes upon the back of
a beautiful horse. One of the quaintest exhibitions I ever saw was that of trained geese and
herons, whose awkward motions made their little
"act" extremely comical. Could some fancier
manage to get a company of cranes to execute on
the stage the extraordinary dances in which these
and some other birds indulge during the breeding
season, he would make a decided hit.

Probably the most satisfactory results of all
would be obtained from careful tuition of the crow,
which seems to me to stand at the head of the
birds in respect to native intelligence; and it is
curious that so little has been done with him in
this direction.

When we come to the quadrupeds, a great field
is opened to us; but the limits of space require
me to confine my attention to one branch of their
association with man, as illustrating their approach
to him in intellectual power and attributes. Let
me take, then, the "stars" of the menagerie and
variety theatre — the "performing animals" of
the showman.

Highest of these in general organization stand

the four-handed folk, — the apes and monkeys, — among which exists a vast diversity of temperament and tractability. Their emotional nature is highly developed, and this often leads to an uncertainty of temper, and a ferocity combined with enormous strength, as age advances, which interfere sadly with the work of the trainer. The higher anthropoid apes become wholly unmanageable in advanced life. The imitative faculties of monkeys are large, however, and it is these which are cultivated, the teacher adding as much discrimination as he can impart.

It is hard to force these animals to fix their attention upon, or persevere in, any one thing; and it would seem that their minds are too bright, while lacking balance of judgment, for the trick-teacher's purpose. Hence, in shows, nowadays, few monkeys are introduced except as rough-riders upon ponies, where they lend a comical element to the programme of the ring. Formerly their grotesque appearance and gestures were more taken advantage of. In France one may see still (or lately could) a troupe of monkeys managed as a part of a company of small trick animals, in a performance called "The Roman Orgy." The manager was an eccentric genius, M. Corvi. Behind a table well provided with biscuits and nuts sit a row of them, — some dressed as monks, others in military style, and others in the classic toga. A little monkey, with

M

a basket in his hand, dances about the table, waiting upon the company; and the whole affair is very amusing, but not very edifying. Two centuries ago, if the annals of such resorts as Raneleigh Gardens, in London, can be trusted, monkeys were taught accomplishments far in advance of anything in modern shows.

Next in zoölogical rank to the quadrumana, come the carnivora — the wild beasts — lions, tigers, leopards, wild-cats, wolves, dogs, foxes, and jackals; and those of the sea — the seals, sea-lions, etc.

Here culminates the interest of every circus performance. The lion-tamer is king of kings. A man who plays with tigers and juggles with wolves compels us to admire to the utmost the dominance of human courage.

For these wild beasts are controlled wholly by fear. Some men may acquire, for brief periods, a certain influence over a lion or tiger or leopard, but they are never safe — never can be trusted for a moment; and a lion "tamer" is not really one — that is, he is not a person who has changed the disposition of his charges from enmity to friendship, persuading them out of their savagery into a second nature of trust and self-control; he is simply a conqueror who enforces obedience. And how complete is this human dominance when it can force, literally, the lion to lie down with the lamb, and the warring barons of the forest to form a congress of peace and sit in a tableau!

During the World's Fair at Chicago, and for
some years afterward, the principal cities of the
United States were treated to exhibitions of Hagenbeck's remarkable troupes of trained animals.
Hagenbeck was at the head of a firm in Hamburg
which dealt more largely than any other in the
world in living animals for zoölogical gardens
and menageries, and it was natural that he should
produce the excellent exhibition he had organized.
In numbers, variety, and freedom from visible
restraint, these troupes exceeded anything seen
upon the modern stage, though it is likely that
the shows in the ancient Roman arenas equalled
or even exceeded them in both skill and audacity.
The crowning spectacle of each performance was,
as I have hinted, a tableau in which lions and
lionesses, tigers and their mates, leopards, jaguars,
pumas, bears, and now and then other beasts,
wholly unchained, mounted upon stands and arranged themselves into a sort of pyramid, well
worth beholding ; but they were required to keep
this formal position only a few seconds, when
they gladly obeyed the ring-master's permission to
come down and rush away to their dens. But,
after all, interesting as this spectacular " act " was,
it was remarkable only in showing how the most
savage and naturally jealous and quarrelsome
carnivora can be made to keep the peace in each
other's company.

It is doubtful whether lions, tigers, and their

kin have minds developed in a wild state to anything like the degree of those of many of the
smaller, fur-bearing animals, such as the ermine,
fox, or wolverine. They are endowed with so
much agility, strength, and endurance that they
rarely need exercise much thought in securing
their prey; while the caution and cleverness required of the weaker species, in order not only
to get food, but to escape from their enemies,
which sharpen their faculties daily, are uncalled
for in the case of these powerful felines, who
dread no enemies except man.

Why they should feel this awe of man it is
difficult to explain. Neither his size nor his erect
position can account for it, and only in long-set-
tled or much-hunted regions can the power of his
firearms be learned. Captives may dread the
sting of his whip, yet they certainly must be
aware that they might disarm and crush him with
a blow. The explanation probably is that they
are unable to comprehend his habits — to fathom
his mental attitude — to learn what he is likely
to do next, and are awed by the mystery of his
conduct, as we might be by that of a supernatural
being of unknown power who came amongst us
and threatened our liberty and happiness.

The minds of the great carnivora are therefore
little exercised in nature, and do not grow; and,
accustomed to power and to seeing all the denizens
of the forest quail before them, they do not know

what it is to feel a sense of help needed or of favors received. It is perfectly natural, therefore, that almost all trainers should agree that kindness (beyond ordinary fair treatment) is wasted upon them. "A tigress," said one of Barnum's tamers, "is as likely to eat you up after six years of attention on her as after six days, if she thinks she is safe in doing so. You must depend on fear — absolute fear alone. Let the beasts know that you can and will beat them when they deserve it, and they will not hurt you."

The celebrated Bidel once tripped and fell in the cage of a lion with whom he had been working for years, whereupon the brute pounced upon him with scarcely a second's hesitation.

Nevertheless, here, as elsewhere, there are exceptions. European newspapers a few years ago told the story of a German woman who was in the habit of performing with a lion said to be very fond of her. On one occasion, as often before, she placed her head within his jaws, and it was thought her hair tickled him, thus causing him intuitively to close his mouth. So was the poor woman killed. When the lion saw what he had done, down he lay by the body, and refusing to allow it to be removed, declined food, and in three days pined away and died. The story may be true, and if so, records one case against a thousand.

Nerve — that is the great secret of the lion-trainer's success; and ceaseless vigilance is the price of his life. He endeavors first to get acquainted with his charges — to accustom them to his presence and voice. The voice is more to them than the appearance. To enter the cage in a new costume, without first speaking, would be to invite death, for the lions would probably not recognize their master until they heard his voice.

The would-be trainer must study his beasts, doing his best to ascertain their individual characters in order that he may adapt himself to them. A few early prove themselves quite unmanageable; and it is said to be easier to teach an adult captive, fresh from the wilderness, than an animal born and reared in the menagerie. As for the training, it consists, to quote Le Roux, who declares himself giving the words of an expert, "in commanding the lion to perform the exercises which please him; that is to say, to make him execute, from fear of the whip, those leaps which he would naturally take in his wild state."

Barnum's trainer, alluded to above, says that lions are the smartest of wild beasts. "You can train a lion to do the ordinary tricks in trade — jumping through hoops and over gates, standing on his hind legs, and so on — in about five weeks' constant work. In this time-table of wild beasts, you can estimate that it would take a lioness

about a week longer, and a leopard, which comes
next in intelligence to a lion, about six weeks, to
learn the same feats.   The tiger would take seven
or eight weeks; a tigress, eight or nine weeks."

Lions have been taught to ride on horseback
and on a tricycle, draw a chariot, to form living
tableaux by grouping themselves together, some
upon the backs of others, etc.; but it is said that
the most difficult feat of all is to teach a wild
beast to let *you* lie upon it.   This used to be
done every night during one of Barnum's tours,
but the performer said the tigress underneath
him was never contented with it.

Though the trainers prefer to give their exhibitions just after the beasts have been fed, this
is often impracticable and does not make much
difference.   The danger lies in the instinct of
ferocity, not in a desire for food; and it often
happens that performances in travelling shows
are given with animals which have not been fed
for two or three days.   There is this difference
between the ferocity of a lion and a tiger: the
former will attack its master now and then out
of spite or temper, while the tiger seizes him
through sheer love of blood.   All tigers are
"man-eaters" if they dare to be.

Lions have been a part of public shows since
history began.   They were led as trophies in the
"triumphs" of semi-barbarians, and were exhibited and sacrificed by thousands in the Roman·

amphitheatre. Six hundred were provided by Pompey for a single festival.

It was with the idea of reviving something of the glory of those old shows that an arrangement was made at the Paris Hippodrome, recently, for the exhibition of lions upon a grand scale. Instead of a cage mounted upon a wagon, these bold managers proposed an arena, and in place of one lion a score.

When the time comes in the programme for the introduction of this "act," the hippodrome is cleared, and the audience awaits in tense silence what is to come. Suddenly, out of the ground arises a palisade of sharp iron pickets twenty feet high and curved inward at their top. It encloses an oval fifty yards long and twenty yards wide. The moment it ceases to rise, and stands fixed in its slot, an opening appears in the centre where flooring has been removed, and half a dozen men, dressed like Roman gladiators, and each bearing a whip and a steel trident, enter by a little gate. They shut this securely behind them, and take their positions. They are none too soon, for already, pushed upward upon a platform-elevator, which rises like a stage-trap in a theatre to fill the central opening, are coming a drove of lions and lionesses. They growl and roar as their great manes and restless bodies rise above the surface, arousing the greetings of the audience.

The instant the platform rests they leap off, rush over to the palisade, and follow one another around it in a swift, creeping trot, seeking some outlet, and now and then pausing with upraised heads to gaze through the thick bars or to examine whether it may be possible to leap over that bristling hedge. This is their first, natural, invariable behavior — their march of display, like the grand procession that begins the circus.   Not until it has been done, not until they have let themselves be seen as they might look when stealing through the twilight of the desert, not until they have again satisfied themselves that they cannot escape, do the trainers crack their whips, call them by name, and put the huge beasts clustering about their feet through the leapings, groupings, and various familiar tricks they have been instructed in.   When the programme has been finished the lions return to the platform and sink out of sight.

The same thing has been seen more lately in the United States, except that the dramatic entrance upon a rising platform was dispensed with, and the brutes came bounding into the arena through a side door in the palisade.

Trained elephants probably come next to these great cats in popular esteem; but none of their show tricks, in my opinion, evince their sagacity as well as the feats they do in the Orient for some useful purpose, under the tutelage of the native mahouts, especially in moving and piling timber.

The elephant has been called by many students of his character the most intelligent of all beasts. Whether he is entitled to this distinction is a question still undecided, but it is to my mind an evidence of high intelligence on their part that they are reluctant to practise stage-tricks which must seem to any self-respecting animal in the highest degree foolish. That elephants have a very keen sense of dignity and propriety is plain. They are influenced by kindness, susceptible of insult and ridicule, and remember for a long time an injury, seeking steadily a safe opportunity to avenge it upon the person who did them the harm. They take great pride in their trappings and proficiency and are jealous of rivals. This feeling an intelligent trainer will take advantage of.

African elephants, by the way, are said to show little aptitude for tricks; but this may be a false observation due to the fact that very few African elephants have been available for experiment, in modern times, at least. Probably the tamed and trained elephants of ancient times were mainly of the African species.

The first of the elephant's lessons is to stay in the ring and walk around it without running away. Some elephants show early that they never can be persuaded not to bolt, whereupon their schooling is abandoned; and all are prone to stop their tricks abruptly and go out — no doubt in disgust at the uselessness of it all.

When the animal has learned to stay in the ring, and to walk obediently wherever he is directed, his weight and personal idiosyncrasies are taken into consideration in deciding what he shall do next ; and the list of things a well-instructed troupe will do in a modern menagerie is long and varied. Take for example the young — and hence light and comparatively nimble — Indian elephants exhibited first in Europe a few years ago, and later shown in circuses and theatres in this country, where they are still (1897) on exhibition, the star of whom is " Boney."

At a signal from hand or whip one will lie down to permit another to place the fore feet on his prostrate body ; or, mounting upon short pillars, some three feet in height, they will stand on their fore legs or on their hind legs alone, or on the two legs of one side, or the two diagonal legs. Not only do they march to music in a manner burlesquing the action of a circus horse, but will play on a hand-organ and a drum simultaneously. The couple then dine at a table, ring violently for a second course, and pay the bill in the most courteous manner.

But the most interesting part of the performance, as I saw it, is that in which they show that their intelligence or their schooling (or both together) has led them to overcome that fear of movable objects which is apparently innate in all elephants, and due, no doubt, to an appreciation of their great weight. To quote a concise and authentic account :

" A cylindrical barrel being placed on its side on the stage, one of the elephants mounted on to it, its four feet being close together, and then, preserving its equilibrium, it moved the feet so as to cause the barrel to roll with it to the opposite side of the stage. This was done without any hesitation on the part of the animal, or enforcement on that of the manager. But the most astounding performance was a game at seesaw, played by the two animals. A strong trestle was placed in the centre of the stage ; across this was laid a stout beam, oscillating freely up and down, its centre resting on the trestle. Going to that end of the beam that was resting on the ground, one of the animals walked up it to the centre, and then, preserving its equilibrium, it rocked the beam up and down. . . . Still more remarkable was the seesawing of the two animals at the same time ; sometimes they were on the narrow beam with their heads in the same direction ; then placing themselves facing one another at the opposite ends, they swayed their big bodies to and fro with such regularity of rhythm that the seesawing took place with considerable rapidity. It was most singular to see these two enormous animals swinging with as much freedom and ease as two children on a plank across a prostrate tree."

Mr. Adam Forepaugh, Jr., explained some time

ago to a New York *Sun* reporter how some of these antics were taught. To make an elephant stand on his hind legs, he is first lifted by an apparatus of ropes and pulleys, until he ascertains what is expected of him. The military drills and so-called dances in figure are acquired by repeated rehearsals with men to guide them, but he does not keep time with the music, as he seems to do — it keeps time with him.

To make him stand on a barrel or roll it is simply a matter of inducing him to remain there; the balancing he attends to himself. The same is true of the seesawing, which begins with a plank flat on the ground. In order to teach an elephant cycling, he is first placed on a wooden arrangement, with his feet in the right position. When he is acquainted with this he is advanced to the tricycle itself, which is held steady until he has taken his place, when the blocks are removed, the pedals go round under his tread, and he soon knows that he will not fall and is expected to work them.

These methods are very simple, but several months of time, expended in short and frequently repeated lessons, delivered with great patience, and without missing a day, must be given to instruction, in order to make a success of it. The brevity of the lessons is an important consideration. What is to us no appreciable exertion at all requires an effort in the mind of an animal which soon wearies it, and makes it both incapable and unreceptive of further instruction until it has rested. This is a fact worth remembering by amateurs who teach tricks to their pets, and often err by lessons too long continued.

In the *St. Nicholas* magazine for February, 1882, appeared a valuable article upon " Men-and-Animal Shows," in which the following remarkable statement is made ; I have never known of its parallel : " During the winter of 1881, a number of elephants were in training at Bridgeport, Conn., for the summer campaign of Mr. P. T. Barnum. They submitted, from day to day, with vast grumbling and trumpeting, to have one leg or another tied up, and be driven around on what they had left. They lay down ; got up ; obeyed every order of the teacher as well as ever they could ; carefully imitated one another ; but their great sagacity was shown after the animals were left a little to themselves. The keepers observed them on their exercise ground, with no human teacher near to offer a word of suggestion or explanation, and yet, singly or in pairs, the huge scholars gravely repeated their lessons, and did their 'practising' on their own account. This was the secret of the wonderful proficiency they afterward exhibited in the ring."

These facts, which I have verified, form quite the most noteworthy evidence I have ever learned in regard to animal intelligence as affected by special training. It seems to me better than the often-observed behavior of riderless troop-horses, which join their squadron, or even another, and perform all the evolutions at command of the bugle as though guided by a rider. Here their naturally gregarious tendencies are only confirmed and regulated by discipline, for they are acting in concert with a great number of fellows.

The performing horses of the circus never fail to win admiration; and the training of what are called waltzing horses appears to have greatly improved of late. Still, that must have been a very striking programme carried out before Louis XIII, where horses danced upon their hind legs to the music; but here again, as in the case of elephants, it was the musicians who kept time with the horses, and not the horses with the playing.

The horse has often been named by enthusiastic lovers of this noble-hearted friend and servant of mankind the most intelligent of animals. Naturalists deny this. They assert that in some faculties, as memory, his brain is marvellously endowed. He is kind in disposition, grateful and quick to respond to what he understands; but in a wild state he shows little intellect, and outside of a very limited range of ideas is dense and slow. No animal is more liable to fits of unreasoning panic, when he forgets the lessons of a lifetime, and will dash headlong against a stone wall or over a precipice without a thought of where he is going.

One of the greatest modern trainers of performing horses is the Frenchman Loyal.   He makes no
secret of his methods, which have often been published — latest in that curious and entertaining
book by Le Roux and Garnier, "Acrobats and
Mountebanks."

The horse, in the opinion of this experienced
man, is one of the dullest animals created ; it has
but one faculty — memory.   It must be forced to
learn its tricks, which are imprinted on its memory by the whip if it resist, and by presents of
carrots if it obey.   These are associated in its
mind with certain words or gestures, and it goes
through the list from fear of punishment on one
hand, and in hope of reward on the other.   This
is certainly different behavior from the lively interest taken by horses in racing, fox-hunting and
cattle-herding, the active obedience and self-dis-
cipline of war chargers or of the steeds used by
firemen ; but in these and similar instances the
animal, naturally gregarious and accustomed to
compete with his fellows, is doing what seems
natural to him, and his exertions have an object
and result that he can comprehend.   The feats of
the circus, on the contrary, depend for their popu-
larity largely in forcing the animal to do what is
contrary to his nature, such as strutting about on
his hind legs, poising himself on pedestals where
there is scarcely room for his feet, lying down to
be tramped upon by his master or mistress, balanc-

ing upon a narrow pathway in imitation of an
equilibrist, and other things — the more out of the
way, the better in the estimation of the populace
— in which a horse can take no interest, and in
doing which he must lose that self-respect and
pride so manifest in him under better circumstances.   While these feats are astonishing, they
are rarely graceful or agreeable to the better
taste.

The ring-master of Barnum and Bailey's present
circus makes a very picturesque arrangement of a
large number of trained horses which group themselves about him upon a stand consisting of a cir-
cular series of rising steps, where the horses stand
facing toward the top, their fore feet resting upon
the next higher step in front of them; after which
they move rapidly round and round, the line upon
each step heading a different way from that above
and below it.   This is a very attractive, but not
a particularly difficult "act," deriving its worth
mainly from the large number of free horses that
act in unison.

Any horse, according to M. Loyal, can be
trained by judicious force; yet certain breeds,
as the Arabian horses and those from Old Prussia,
are easier to teach than any others, and the age is
of great importance.   The best education is received between the fifth and seventh years of the
animal's life; before that the horse is too excita-
ble; afterward, likely to be stiff.

N

The intelligence and cunning of mules are surprising. Few, however, have been trained to perform in public. The donkey, on the contrary, has been the clown's accompanist for centuries, caricaturing his nobler brethren of the ring, as his master caricatures the ring-masters and gymnasts. Twice within a few years troupes of asses have been exhibited, performing in concert most of the feats usually taught to horses, and doing them quite as well. The male ass is regarded as a dangerous animal, however. His gaudy halter is really a strong muzzle to prevent his biting, and his hoofs are never shod, for he is likely to kick at times when it is not his cue to do so. Lately a good deal has been done toward domesticating and training to harness the zebra — that is, Burchell's zebra; but though this has met with considerable success in South Africa, the zebra takes no part in the show-ring as yet beyond drawing a wagon now and then.

Even bulls have been put into the show-tent. An old book records that in 1270 oxen were exhibited in England which could ride on horseback. During the summer of 1883, two young bulls were performing at the Westminster Aquarium in London, whose docility was at least remarkable for novelty. They marched and countermarched, stood upon pedestals, operated the seesaw, walked up and down stairs, fired pistols and rang bells by pulling cords with their mouths, and one jumped over the other's back. These were young animals, but whether they improved as they grew older, or, instead, became stolid and unwieldy, I am not informed. Performing bulls equal to them in extent of programme, at least, have been exhibited in the United States more recently and are still to be seen.

The natural agility of goats has often been taken advantage of by trainers, who have taught them to climb precarious structures and to stand on the tops of bottles, and in other ticklish situations. This is in pursuance of the rule that all trainers ought to follow, namely, to make an animal do difficult things only in the line of his inherent abilities. The goat is a natural climber and equilibrist, or he never could have been taught to walk an ordinary and legitimate tight rope, as one did nightly in London some time ago.

Clowns often exercise the bear and pig in public. Two or three centuries ago, trick-bears were constantly travelling about Europe. The bear exhibits great ingenuity and wit in his native forest; but trainers say he is one of the hardest and most unsatisfactory animals to teach.

The educated pig is a more modern addition to the theatrical menagerie. No animal looks more stupid, but every farmer can tell you this is an error. The wiles and sagacity of the animal in a wild state, or when allowed to run loose and

root in the forests or fields, are the subjects of
many anecdotes. They have been trained in
several instances to scent and point game-birds
like a dog; and have been a feature at country
fairs in Great Britain for many years, picking
out letters of the alphabet as they were called,
and forecasting the fortunes of rustic damsels by
selection of cards.

The French clown Corvi, of whom I spoke
a little while ago, trained pigs effectually, and
says that it requires extreme patience and tender-
ness of treatment. The least touch of the whip
disfigures the tender skin and disgusts the animal with work. Only coaxing succeeds. There
is an Irish proverb which runs thus: "Beat your
wife with a cudgel, and your pig with a straw."

The minor carnivora have furnished the theatre
with several profitable animals, as dogs, cats,
wolves, jackals, hyenas, seals, and others.

Of the dog we would expect a great deal under
the tutelage of a practical teacher of animal tricks,
and the public, perhaps, has not been disappointed,
though to the naturalist the result does not seem
very extensive or encouraging. Of all animals, it
is the one most closely associated with man, and
probably has the deepest insight into the human
mind — quite as deep, perhaps, as we have into
the canine mind. Through unnumbered genera-
tions of special breeding, his inclinations have
been modified toward those things in which he

serves his human masters, and his mind, accustomed to the complexity of human methods, is ripe to acquire new ideas.

In fact, it cannot be too strongly urged that the work of the sheep-herding collie, of the dogs used in finding, attracting, or retrieving game, in discovering truffles, in rescuing lost or drowning persons, etc., exhibit far more real brain-power, sagacity, and true education than all of the accomplishments of trick-dogs put together. These latter are merely doing over and over a routine of things of no real importance or object, and which, as they are always precisely the same, call for nothing more than memory and willingness on the part of the performers; whereas the work of a shepherd's or drover's dog, of a setter on the shooting-ground, and of many other dogs in the service of mankind, requires a constant exercise of judgment, discrimination, and adaptability, and furnishes an incessant stimulus to their minds. No automaton could serve their purpose; and could they not accommodate their conduct intelligently to their master's movements and to constantly varying circumstances, they would be comparatively useless. Any sportsman or herder will tell you that *good sense* is the most essential quality in his four-footed assistant. As a matter of fact, trick-dogs are usually chosen from breeds that are good for nothing else.

This introduces a general and, I believe, a just

criticism of most, if not all, the exhibitions of trained animals seen in modern days; namely, that the "tricks" they are taught are in themselves trivial and without any purpose likely to interest or reward the performer. They tend to stultify rather than improve the animal's mind; and, so far from being marvels of intelligence, rarely show even the extent of the natural capabilities discernible by an appreciative eye in the untrained animal. The truth is the trainer is exhibiting himself, not his animals, and it is the teacher rather than his pupils that we ought to admire.

Wolves have always been regarded as nearly intractable; but that they could be both tamed and trained has been shown within the past few years by a French trainer who had a pack that would perform like dogs. The hyena, too, is taught tricks, but it is said to require a long time and many lessons to force anything into his head. Seals, on the contrary, are docile, and are taught to do a number of feats which derive their interest mainly from seeing the attempts of such awkward animals to do what a dog or cat would do naturally and easily. They show, at any rate, bright minds and great docility.

A pretty young woman lately caused much interest in Paris by an exhibition of trained rabbits, and Mademoiselle Claire's white pets seemed greatly to enjoy their mimicry of the big elephants of the circus. A series of illustrations shows a rabbit sitting on top of a long paper cylinder or tunnel, supported upon a stick, while a procession of bunnies bolts incontinently through it. Just below, a clown-rabbit is seen jumping through a paper drum, while another circus rabbit fires a pistol, and still a third drags a miniature chariot around the arena. While a dissipated little creature stands on his head and shows other signs of over-indulgence, another pet rocks gently to and fro in a little swing. Others of Mademoiselle Claire's performers scamper under burning wickets, and vault between blazing candles over a succession of candelabra arranged as hurdles.

This is much prettier than the trained rats and mice which have been shown in the same city of clever people, for all our associations with the rabbit are endearing; and the success that has followed the training of these pets, which do not stand high in brain power, goes to show what I have suggested hitherto, that if its disposition is favorable, a weak-minded animal learns tricks more satisfactorily than a strong-minded one.

With some account of a most interesting troupe of trained cats this essay must come to a close; and this account has been left until the last because it is perhaps the most recent, and one of the most striking of the trainer's triumphs. This troupe is that of the young Dutchman Bonnetty, which formed one of the main attractions of the

Winter Circus at Paris some years ago. These cats were all of a Dutch breed, which Bonnetty says are especially docile; and his method was simply patient persistence in informing the cat what was wanted of it, and persuading it to do that thing. Here whipping and harsh words are of no use. Pussy's nature is quite different from the dog's. If the cat refuses to do what you wish, and cannot be coaxed, violence will only harden her heart. You must simply abandon the matter for that time at least. The hardest work was to teach the first cat. It required months of patient attention. Adding them one by one, he found the training of the late recruits much easier, because they imitated quickly what the older performers were doing. Bonnetty has never been able to succeed in teaching Persian or Angora cats, and does not find kittens much more ready to learn than full-grown cats. He says, also, that some cats, able and willing to go through their antics well in private, cannot be induced to attempt them amid the noise and glare of the circus.

There were fifteen or twenty cats in his troupe. When the curtain rose a flock of canaries was seen perched upon a cord stretched across the stage. Near them some white mice and dappled gray rats were resting quietly. M. Bonnetty opened the door of the cats' palace, and in Indian file all the artists marched slowly out, striding over the rodents and birds, some of which flew off and fear-

lessly returned, alighting on the heads of the cats.
They caught these little animals, their natural
prey, and played with them, holding them in
their paws, and even in their teeth, without doing
them the slightest injury; they jumped through
a blazing hoop held up by the trainer, made sur-
prisingly long leaps over hurdles; turned summer-
saults, and did other gymnastic exercises on the
backs of thirty-two chairs placed in a row;
marched around in time to music like little soldiers, and grouped themselves in many graceful
and comical attitudes. In all these capers the
pussies, who live a life of royal comfort and in-
dulgence, seemed to enjoy themselves as much as
if the whole affair were a spontaneous frolic;
but it is noteworthy that these trained cats, while
tamed to a very unusual degree by their kind,
patient, and persistent master, must be kept strictly
captive, since otherwise they would run away
upon those nocturnal expeditions in which the
house pet becomes once more the wild cat, taking
to the roofs and back fences of the city only because there is no jungle convenient; and M. Bonnetty has lost two or three of his best performers
by such escapades.

Their education and training, after all, is only
skin deep — an acquired polish affecting character
to only a small degree. This is true of nearly the
whole menagerie, which lives at best an artificial
life; and nowadays I rarely go to see it.

A WOODLAND CODGER

THE porcupine is one of the queerest, and by no means the prettiest, of our sylvan friends. His broad, lumpish body, twice the bigness of a woodchuck, is modelled upon the shape of an egg; the nose is blunt, the legs are short, and one wonders how this Falstaff of the woods can scramble over the rocks and up and down trees as well as he does. But for something to laugh at, get the queer little codger to sit up on his hams, with his tail planted behind, like one foot of a tripod.

He seems truly a witless, slow, unsociable beast, working at night for the most part, more from churlishness than for any practical reason, minding his own business, and insisting that his neighbors attend strictly to theirs. He may even be quarrelsome when interfered with, and Shakespeare hit it, as usual, when he characterized the porcupine as "fretful." He will never take the trouble to be aggressive; but he knows he is well prepared, and resists an enemy with such vigor that he is rarely overcome. He is much better armed than

THE CANADA PORCUPINE.

the European porcupine, whose forward parts are so largely unprotected that a wolf or a big cat need only be agile enough to seize or strike the head in order to kill it, while our subject is completely clothed with stiff quills, which, by their peculiar construction, form as efficient an armor as do the more solid shields of the armadillo, — more efficient, in fact, since a jaguar or puma will simply crush a small armadillo and eat it, shell and all, as a man might an almond; whereas, the longer a wild-cat gnaws at the urson (as Buffon called it), the greater its discomfiture, even when, as sometimes happens, he succeeds·in devouring the prickly meal. This very week, I have read an account of a lynx, ravenous with hunger, to judge by its empty stomach and very gaunt appearance, found dead beside a stricken porcupine, its mouth full of quills, one of which, in its struggles to rub them out, the creature had pushed through its eye into its brain. Here is a tragedy of the woods.

These quills are intermixed with long, brownish black hair, which here and there grows in tufts, and on the back and sides is sometimes eight inches long, but on the belly and inside of the limbs forms a dense fur. The hair of the nose changes almost insensibly into short spines, an inch or less long, which gradually increase to a length of four or five inches on the haunches and tail. They are white, tipped with blackish brown, as a rule, but not banded like those of the Old

World species. All the quills, which are in reality only modified hairs, and are hollow and rigid like the stems of feathers, point backwards and ordinarily lie close to the body, but may be erected by the voluntary action of muscles underlying the skin. This done, their points stand out on every side, presenting a *chevaux-de-frise* within which the animal squats as secure as one of the Highland squares at Waterloo.

The self-inflating spiny globe-fishes and the hedgehog (not to speak of thorny invertebrates, such as the sea-urchins, murices, etc.) enjoy a similar defence; but the porcupine's armament is superior to any of these, for it is offensive as well as defensive.

It is a long-discredited fable, of course, that the porcupine shoots his spines at a tormentor, just as we no longer believe that it lays eggs or brings water in its quills to its young; but the seed of truth in the matter is the fact that the quills are so loosely attached to the flesh as to be readily detached, and in fact some may be flirted out when the animal shakes himself vigorously — something he never does if he can avoid it. Moreover, each spine is needle-pointed, and minutely but strongly barbed, so that it sticks in whatever touches it, and is immediately withdrawn from the skin. Thus any animal that leaps upon or bites a porcupine finds its paws, shoulders, and mouth full of detached quills, which so divert its attention for some time to come that it rarely notices the escape of its would-be victim. Every movement of the muscles causes them to penetrate deeper; and there seems no limit to their inflammatory and often fatal travels. Dr. Merriam says that he has found them everywhere in animals that he has dissected, once discovering a whole quill between the two leg bones of the hind limb of a fisher. Nevertheless, the porcupine is occasionally attacked and killed by panthers, wild-cats, wolves, martens, eagles, and owls, but this usually happens, probably, under the stress of extreme hunger and in winter, as in the case related a moment ago. Few dogs seem to have sense enough to let him alone; and it is because so many of these are injured that hunters regard the porcupine as vermin, and kill it at every opportunity.

But the animal is not content merely to curl up and let an enemy come to grief upon his defences, for he possesses in his thick, triangular, muscular tail, along the sides of which grow the stiffest and strongest of quills, a powerful weapon for active warfare. I was once, with a friend, climbing one of the Catskill peaks, when we ran across a porcupine and quickly cornered it in a nook of rocks. Ducking its head between its fore feet, swelling up and turning its back upon us, it instantly bristled all over until it looked like a big ripe chestnut burr. Its tail seemed to offer a sort of handle, however, and before I could remonstrate, my friend reached forward for it. He had not fairly touched it before he leaped back with a howl of surprise and pain, and held up a hand stuck as full as a pin-cushion with glistening spines, which the beast had planted with a lightning-like flirt of its tail. I thought I heard the old codger chuckle in unison with my laughing sympathy as I pulled the prickles out of the smarting hand, but it lay still and kept its tender nose well out of the reach of a club. We had no wish to kill it, however, but wanted to learn more of the creature's skill with the broadsword, and taking a stick, gently touched the tail again. It responded by a sideways jerk of surprising quickness and force, knocking the stick aside and dropping a few quills; but it did not hurl its whole body, as Audubon describes; nor did the caudal spines themselves rattle loudly, as the longer ones of the European species do.

A brief quotation from Darwin's book on " Expression " will describe this peculiarity of the Old World porcupine to the best advantage:

" Porcupines rattle their quills and vibrate their tails when angered ; and one behaved in this manner when a live snake was placed in the compartment. The quills on the tail are very different from those on the body ; they are short, hollow, thin like a goose-quill, with their ends transversely truncated, so that they are open ; they are supported on long, thin, elastic foot-stalks. Now when the tail is rapidly shaken, these hollow quills

strike against each other and produce . . . a peculiar continuous sound. We can, I think, understand why porcupines have been thus provided,
through the modification of their protective spines,
with this special, sound-producing instrument.
They are nocturnal animals, and if they scented
or heard a prowling beast of prey, it would be a
great advantage to them, in the dark, to give warning to their enemy what they were and that they
were furnished with dangerous spines."

One now sees how aptly the fellow is named
"porcupine,"—a corruption of the Old French
words *porc espin*, meaning "spiny pig." This, in
fact, seems to have been the original import of
the Latin *hystrix*,—the family name, derived
from a Greek compound noun signifying "hairy
pig." The Spanish, Portuguese, and Italians use
substantially the same term, while the German
nations have translated it into *stachelschwein*,
stekel-vark, etc., meaning "stickle-hog." The
early English spellings and quaint variants, such
as porcupig, forkentine, purpentine, and the like
are innumerable. Buffon's term, *l'urson*, was a
rather fantastic figment, intended to indicate by
the first syllable that it resembled a bear's cub,
and, by the second, to remind one that its home
was about the bay of Hudson, for whom Buffon
professed great admiration.

The porcupine is a denizen of the woods and
rarely leaves them for the farmers' fields, while

o

it is unknown on Western prairies, though in the
Southwest the Pacific Coast species is sometimes
seen far from the sparse groves along the rivers.
In spite of senseless persecution, it is still common throughout the Northeastern States and Canada, wherever forests remain, and in favorable
districts has really increased of late. In such
places, the lumberman or fisherman, camping in
some glade, is sure to be visited by these guests,
who come blundering about his quarters at midnight, nosing around the doorway for something
to eat, and if he is sleeping in a tent, often getting entangled in the guy-ropes or making general
trouble by an attempt to push their way under the
canvas. Mr. E. P. Bicknell relates that when he
was encamped on the summit of Slide Mountain,
the loftiest in the Catskills, in 1882, his cabin was
besieged by porcupines all night long, and that
"their dark forms could be seen moving about
among the shadows in the moonlight, while their
sharp cries and often low conversational chatter,
singularly like the voices of infants, were weird
interruptions of the midnight silence." Mr. Bicknell adds that their temerity seemed natural fool-
ishness rather than courage, and that it was
impossible to drive them out of the camp for any
length of time ; even when one had been shot,
while trying to bore its way into the tent, another
repeated the attempt beside the dead body of its
companion. Their great love of salt is probably

the special attraction that brings them to camps, where the scraps of bacon-rind and table-crumbs would be tidbits of the highest excellence in their estimation. It appears to be extremely fond of sweets, also, gnawing old sugar-barrels and maple-sugar utensils, and being especially fond of maple bark. A. Leith Adams, the author of "Field and Forest Rambles" (in New Brunswick), informs us that they eat the tips of the cast antlers of deer, which are rarely found unharmed by their incisors; and he also mentions the extraordinary size of their ordure, which is often mistaken for that of deer.

The porcupine's natural food, however, is vegetable, and mainly bark and browse, in search of which it spends most of its time in trees, although seemingly as awkwardly built and accoutred for such a life as well could be; but the toes have very long and strong claws, good for clinging. It is true, however, that our Northern species pursues an arboreal life much less exclusively than do the tropical American species, being intermediate in habits as well as structure between the Old World terrestrial species and the South American tree-porcupines.

These tree-porcupines (genus Synetheres), of which eight or ten species are spread from Mexico to Paraguay, are far better fitted for climbing, and are almost exclusively arboreal. They are smaller and lighter than the Canada porcupine, have, short, close, many-colored spines, and a long, tapering, distinctly prehensile tail, that forms a fifth hand equal to that of the monkey or opossum. The soles of their feet, too, are provided with a peculiar fleshy pad on the inner side, " between which and the toes boughs and other objects can be firmly grasped." Two of them — the couiy and the coendou — are familiar to the people of Guiana, Brazil, and Bolivia ; and, in the former, the spines — which may be erected — are ordinarily covered by long gray hairs, which, we are told, effectually conceal the animal from the notice of predatory birds, as it lies asleep during the day, heaped up in an indistinguishable mass in the fork of some moss-draped tree. Of the coendou, in the island of Trinidad, a curious fact is recorded by Mr. Frank M. Chapman, Bulletin Am. Mus. Nat. Hist., Vol. V, p. 227, as follows :

"The presence of this arboreal species [*Synetheres prehensilis*] is made known by the nauseating odor it gives forth. This is especially noticeable in the early morning when the air is humid and before the daily trade-winds begin to blow. In walking through the forests at this time, it was not unusual to encounter odoriferous strata of air proceeding from individuals of this species. So dense, however, was the parasitic vegetation on the trees in which they conceal themselves, that they were practically invisible from below.

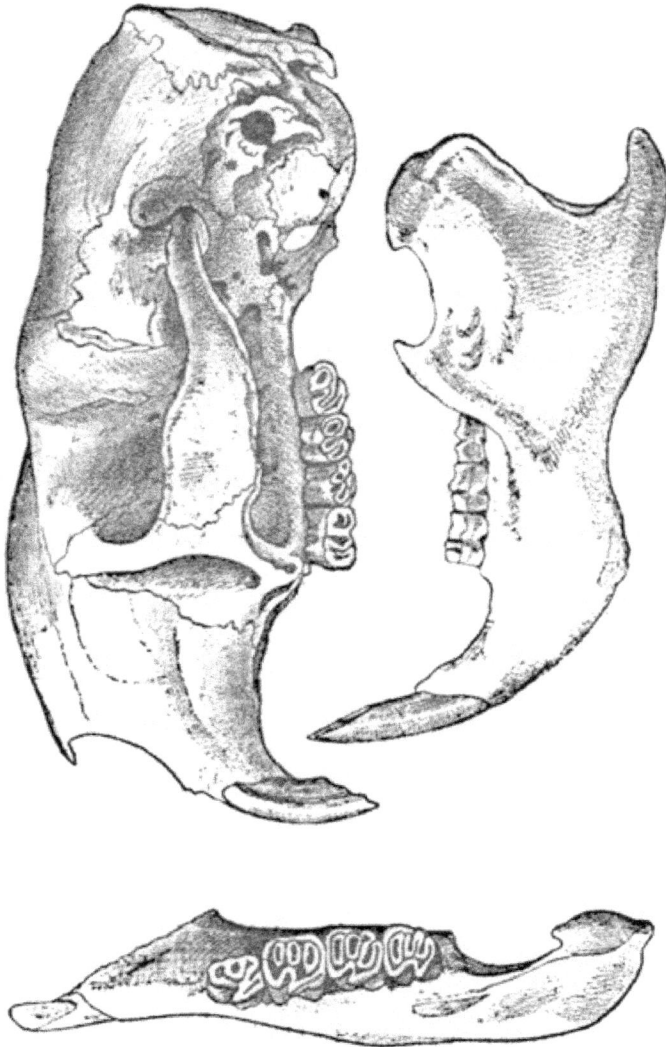

SKULL OF THE PORCUPINE. — Natural size. After Baird.

Whether suited or unsuited to the life, the Northern porcupine spends much of his time aloft, sometimes remaining for weeks in a single big tree, usually a hemlock. Curled up in some deep fork or hollow, he dozes away the daylight, and at night feeds upon twigs and leaves. Beginning at the topmost spray, he will gnaw and clip away every bit of fresh bark, sprouting twig and leaf, and circle regularly downward, taking each branch in succession out to its very tip, despite his weight and awkwardness, by pulling the outermost twigs within reach of his orange teeth, and continuing until the whole tree has been despoiled of every edible particle. Then, having literally eaten himself out of house and home, he chooses another tree and repeats the process. Sometimes he knows of better quarters in some hollow close by, and goes and comes nightly; but having found a tree-pasture to his purpose, he rarely leaves it until it has been denuded. This is more true of the winter, however, than the summer, for the animal does not hibernate, though spells of extremest cold render him temporarily inactive. Hearne says that in the far North the Indians frequently leave them in a tree "till a more convenient season," confident that when they want them they can find them. The species inhabits British America and Alaska as far north as the forests extend.

Yet they travel about somewhat, as is betrayed by their baby-like footprints. They are flat-footed or plantigrade, like a bear, and the soles are naked, but along their sides and between the toes grows a thick fringe of long coarse hair, which acts like snow-shoes in sustaining the animal's weight on the snow, in which its low-hung body leaves a deep rut as it tramps along. The hemlock, sugar-maple, basswood, ash, and slippery elm in the East, and in the West the cottonwood, are its favorites, these having a thick, juicy underbark. Its depredations occasionally kill trees, especially its habit of girdling them, but the total of damage in this way is trifling. Sometimes, in winter, it invades the orchard and gnaws the bark from young orchard trees or despoils a nursery, but the harm thus done is never very great.

In summer the porcupine wanders more widely and enjoys a more varied fare, eating young leaves and buds of shrubs, herbage, and many roots and vegetables. Dr. Merriam mentions their fondness for lily-pads in the Adirondacks and tells us that they sometimes quarrel for possession of a stranded log by which these dainties may be reached, snarling, growling, and pushing one another away or even into the water, but not biting, although their great front teeth might inflict serious wounds. In the fall, mast, and especially beechnuts, forms a staple article of diet, as with other large rodents. He is fond of apples, Indian corn, etc., which he eats sitting up on his haunches, holding the morsel up to his mouth like a squirrel.

The animal can hardly be said to have a home;
but he uses a hollow tree as a tenement, or even a
hole among the rocks. As warm weather approaches, the female produces two or three young,
which, according to Dr. Merriam, are monstrous
for the size of the mother. They are actually
larger, he assures us, and relatively more than
thirty times larger, than the young of the black bear
at birth. The female has four pectoral mammæ.

Their flesh is eaten by the Indians, but has
never been liked by white men. The use of the
quills in ornamentation by our Indians is well
known, robes, garments, moccasins, belts, pouches,
weapon-cases, baskets, and everything else being
ornamented with them by the squaws with great
skill and often with truly artistic effect; but as
usual the earliest methods and patterns, when the
Indians used their own delicate dyes and sinew
threads, were much better than is seen in these
days of aniline colors and crude imitations of the
white man's art. The application may be made in
any of three or four ways, as, by weaving or sew-
ing the quill into the texture of the object itself;
by winding it transversely about the thread that
forms the *appliqué* pattern; by interweaving it
with the strands of a basket or lashing; or by glu-
ing it upon the surface. The native South Americans did not practise this art, although they made
a somewhat similar use of bird-quills, as, on the
other hand, was not done in the northern continent.

No similar utilization seems to have been made of the quills of the European porcupine, although the longest ones are turned into fancy penholders; and in India and Malaya they weave little baskets, etc., out of them, which are often as pretty as they are strange.

Reviewing its narrow life, the strongest impression left upon one's mind seems to be that of the creature's sluggishness and stupidity. These are perhaps concomitants, if not consequences, of its strictly vegetarian life, in which its tastes are so simple that it rarely seems to have to make the least exertion for food at any season of the year; and of a highly protected condition, which makes it careless of danger, and hence unvigilant and steadily inclined to sluggishness of mind as well as of body. It is not well for an animal to be too safe or too comfortable, for its mind grows rusty with disuse, or, if it never had use, lies inert and the whole creature exists on a low plane. I do not know another animal of the American woods that is so well off and so uninteresting as the Canada porcupine.

The porcupines are the central figures in a group of rodents, called after them Hystricomorpha. This group is one of the sections of the suborder of Simplicidentates, which have only two upper teeth (incisors) in front, instead of four, as in the picas and rabbits (Duplicidentates); and it contains eight families, some of which are extinct, including many rat-like animals, small and large, some belonging to North Africa, but mostly South American.

In many members of this group the hair has a peculiar sharpness, with more or less intermixture of stiff prickly hairs, becoming quills in the most typical ; while others, as the chinchilla and coypu, are noted for the extreme softness of their fur, making it valuable in trade.

The central family is that of the porcupines (Hystricidæ), long ago divided into two branches : — the synetherine, or New World arboreal porcupines, and the hystricinine, or Old World terrestrial porcupines ; but this division is made on anatomical grounds, not upon difference of habitat or habits, to which the classifiers are more blind than is always well for the stability of their work. To the former branch belong our subject and its South American cousins, the tree-porcupines ; to the latter, the common European porcupine.

Of the last named (*Hystrix cristata*) a brief account by W. S. Dallas may be useful for purposes of comparison with the characteristics of the American form.

"The head, shoulders, limbs, and under parts are clothed with short spines intermixed with hairs usually of a dusky or brownish black hue ; the neck is marked with a whitish collar ; from the back of the head and neck there arises a great crest of long bristles, many of them fifteen or sixteen inches in length, which can be elevated and depressed at the pleasure of the animal, are gently curved backwards, and are either dusky with the extremities white, or whitish throughout; the hinder portion of the body is entirely covered by a great number of long sharp spines, ringed with black and white, but always having the extremities white. These spines vary considerably in size, some of them being very long (fifteen or sixteen inches), comparatively slender and flexible; others shorter (from six to twelve inches), but much stouter. . . . The porcupine lives in holes among the rocks, or in a burrow, which he makes for himself in ordinary ground. In this retreat he passes the day in sleep, coming forth in the evening in search of food, which consists of herbage of various kinds, fruits, roots, and the bark and leaves of trees and bushes. He is slow in his movements, and does not even display much activity in burrowing. His habits are solitary, except during the pairing-season; and during the winter he passes most of his time in his habitation, without, however, falling into a torpid state. The pairing takes place early in the year, . . . and in the spring or early summer the female produces from two to four young in a nest carefully lined with leaves, grasses, roots, and other vegetables. The young porcupines are born with their eyes open, and their bodies are covered with short soft spines, which are pressed close to the body. These speedily harden and grow longer, and the young do not appear to remain very long with their mother. The flesh . . . is eaten in the countries where the animal occurs. When pursued or irritated, he stands on the defensive, erects his formidable quills and crest, stamps on the

ground with his hind feet, after the manner of a
hare, jerks himself toward the object of his dread,
as if to wound it with his spines, and at the same
time produces a curious noise, by rattling the open
quills of the tip of his tail."

This animal is still fairly numerous in Greece,
Italy, and Sicily, and formerly ranged throughout
Southern Europe; south of the Mediterranean it
extends from Tunis to Morocco, and southward
into the Soudan.   A closely similar species takes
the place of this one in Syria, and ranges thence
eastward to India, where it injures tank-walls by
its burrowing, and often destroys vegetable crops:
hunting it with dogs is a favorite sport in the hill-
regions.   Four or five smaller species, without
nuchal crests, inhabit northeast India and the
Malayan coasts and islands; and fossil species of
Hystrix belong to the upper Tertiary rocks of
both Asia and Europe.   South Africa has also a
local kind of porcupine.   Lastly, mention must
be made of the brush-tailed porcupines, of the
genus Atherura, two species of which are found
in the Malayan region, and one in West Africa;
they are smaller than the foregoing, and rejoice in
long tails tipped with a bunch of peculiar flattened
scales.   A still more specialized form inhabits
Borneo.   Such are the Old World representatives
of the tribe; and they differ from their New World
cousins more in anatomical peculiarities and an
indisposition to climb trees than in anything else.

Our common porcupine of the eastern United States and Canada (*Erethizon dorsatus*) once ranged over all the forested parts of the country north of Virginia and Kentucky; it seems to reach northward nearly or quite to the limit of forest-growth, having been reported from the Mackenzie valley. Along the Missouri River it mingles sparingly with a second, Western species, the yellow-haired (*Erethizon epixanthus*), which ranges across the Plains to the Rocky Mountains, and to all parts of the Pacific Coast southward as far as the Mexican border. Godman, Audubon, and the older writers, so far as they spoke of this latter animal at all, confused it with the Eastern form.

THE COMMON NORTHERN SKUNK.

VIII

THE SKUNK, CALMLY CONSIDERED

THE skunk is among the handsomest animals
in the fields, and carries himself with an air of
genteel leisure, while he makes no effort to hide
himself from our admiration. He is not much
given to going abroad in daylight, though I have
seen him at high noon; but more frequently you
meet him at twilight, when he is little disposed to
make way for you. "I have come near stepping
upon him," exclaims Mr. Burroughs, "and was
much the more disturbed of the two." If you pay
no attention to him, he will pass, or let you pass,
in dignified indifference, going about his business;
but if you try to stop him, or follow so inquisitively as to alarm him, he will make ready to resent it; and, as the Greeks were to be dreaded
when bearing gifts, so this foe is most to be feared
when it turns tail to the enemy.

Here we are, right at the start, as is inevitable!

When the word "skunk" is mentioned, the first
thought in every one's mind is of the animal's
extraordinary ability in getting himself into bad
odor. Let us take up this matter of the skunk's

fetid discharge at once, therefore, and have done with it.

In the first place, it is to be noted that musky secretions, more or less intense in their nauseating effect on the human nostrils, are characteristic of the whole tribe to which the skunk belongs, — the Mustelidæ. To this tribe belong the European polecat, the mink, — whose discharges, when excited, are far more disgusting than anything the skunk utters, — and various other evil-smelling fur-bearers, while to the closely related badger family belong not only our own far from fragrant badger, but also the stinking-badger or teledu of the East Indies, the honey-badgers of South Africa, and the wolverine. Of this company, — so abominable when considered from this single point of view, —the skunk is by no means the worst, although none equal him in the power of disseminating the perfume, nor in its copiousness. The Yankees call him an "essence pedler."

In the skunk, the fetid material is contained in two capsules embedded in the muscles beneath the root of the tail, one on each side of the intestinal outlet, into which, just within the anus, they open by little nipples perforated by fine ducts; another longer duct leads into each of them from absorbent vessels situated deeper in the body. These glandular capsules are not larger than peas, and are enclosed in a thick envelope of muscles, which, when suddenly and

forcibly contracted by the animal, convert the
capsule, duct, and nipple into a syringe, forcing
its contents out in a thin spurt or double jet,
which may reach more than a dozen feet.
Whether it is possible for the animal to discharge one barrel of his weapon and reserve
the other, I do not know, but I should think
it likely. The liquid is clear yellow in color, and
somewhat phosphorescent, so as to be faintly visible in the dark ; it is intensely acid in its chem-
ical reaction, and virulently acrid toward any
mucous or tender surface upon which it falls.
This, together with its extreme volatility and
offensive odor, makes it almost suffocating when
inhaled in any considerable amount, and, in ex-
cess, it may produce unconsciousness (anæsthesia)
accompanied by difficult breathing and even fatal
results. The odor has the quality of musk, as,
indeed, do nearly all animal discharges of this
nature, whether they come from deer, civets,
musteline animals, or reptiles ; and, when per-
ceived and calmly considered at a reasonable distance, it is by no means unendurable, having a
pungent and, perhaps, disagreeable, but not an
unwholesome smell. The nose is pained and
offended rather than disgusted. The liquid also
resembles musk in its extraordinary volatility.
The total discharge is really a very small quantity, — scarcely more than a large drop, — yet it
will perfume the air for a mile in every direction

in favorable weather, or even more, if we may trust many accounts; and the minutest particle sprayed upon one's clothes will make them entirely unwearable. Its persistence is equally remarkable and embarrassing. No amount of washing or disinfection, short of destroying the fibre of the cloth, suffices to eradicate the taint. Burying them for any practicable time is of no use, for even if the garments seem at first to be free, heat will bring back strong reminders of the wearer's unsavory experience. Where chloride of lime can be used, the smell can be destroyed, but otherwise time alone will rid one of its presence.

The Indians of the Upper Columbia valley, by the way, tell a quaint legend of the origin of this savory characteristic of our subject. A few miles below the mouth of the Spokane River, the banks become rocky walls and are strangely broken. "The rocks take all imaginable forms, showing up as pinnacles, terraces, perpendicular bluffs, devils'-slides, and giants' causeways, — the whole forming one of the most beautiful, grandest sights in the universe." Among these is a grayish-white cone, about five hundred feet high, which is a noted landmark, and concerning which the Indians have a legend, of which the skunk is the hero. It has been written down in his report upon the navigation of the Upper Columbia, made to the War Department by Lieutenant Thomas W. Symons, U.S.A., as follows:

"It would seem that in the long ago a skunk, a coyote, and a rattlesnake each had a farm on top of the Whitestone. Those were the days before the skunk was as odorous as he is now, but was esteemed a good fellow and pleasant companion by other animals. As in some other small communities, jealousies, dissensions, and intrigues arose in this one. The result was that the coyote and the rattlesnake took a mean advantage of the skunk one night when he was asleep, and threw him off the rock, away down into the river. He was not drowned, however, but floated on and on, far away to the south and west, until he came to the mouth of the river, where lived a great medicine man and magician. To him the skunk applied, and was fitted out with an apparatus warranted to give immunity from and conquest over all his enemies. Back he journeyed along the river to his old home, where he arrived, much to the surprise of the coyote and rattlesnake, and commenced to make it so pleasant for them with his pungent perfumery apparatus, the gift of the magician, that they soon left him in undisputed possession of his rocky home, which he has maintained ever since."

It is not surprising to find that this powerful secretion has a marked effect upon our eyes and air-passages whenever it comes into contact with them. When shot into the eye, as has often happened, intense pain and acute inflammation (conjunctivis) follow, and have been known to produce blindness in a few cases, though usually the injury disappears in a week or ten days. The effect upon the throat and lungs of inhaling any considerable quantity of this substance long ago suggested its value as a specific " in certain spasmodic affections of the air-passages, such as asthma, hooping-cough, and asthmatic croup," but it must be used with caution, if at all, since more than one sufferer, while confessing the relief given, has abandoned the remedy as worse than the ailment. Audubon and Bachman tell a funny story of how an asthmatic preacher emptied his church one morning by attempting to take a sniff of the medicine in the pulpit, and somehow losing control of the stopper of the vial. A sequel of this benefit from the gland-substance has been the application of the oil from the fat of the animal to the relief of similar ailments, without any real effect, of course.

Dogs howl with pain when they get a charge full in the face, and rush anywhere in evident agony, plunging their noses into the dust, dragging their faces against the ground, and showing every sign of intense pain. It is doubtful whether the vileness (to us) of the odor has much to do with their distress ; but this point, and its bearings on the question of the value of this discharge as a means of defence, will be considered hereafter.

The animal makes use of its artillery by turning its stern toward the enemy, elevating its tail, and

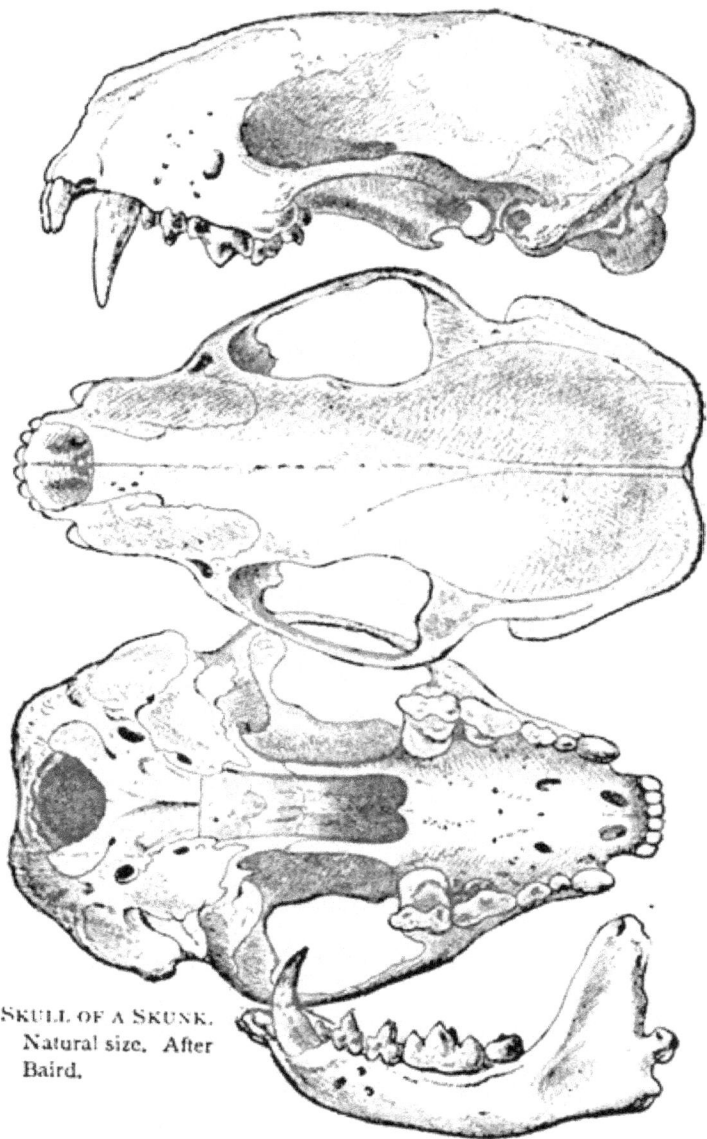

SKULL OF A SKUNK.
Natural size. After
Baird.

raising one of its hind legs. Its aim is taken with the utmost accuracy, and it can repeat the discharge several times, having a magazine gun at command. A simple surgical operation, if made by intelligent hands, will extract these glands, or cut the duct leading from the capsule to the nipple-like orifice, after which the animal is powerless for harm, — a precaution highly judicious in the case of a domesticated example of this species, if one values his peace of mind !

Having thus rendered our subject innocuous, we may now proceed to study him, for he is one of the prettiest and most interesting of all our wild animals.

The skunk is about the size of a cat, but has more nearly the shape of a raccoon, being taller behind than about the fore quarters, and with a pointed, somewhat pig-like snout; this form, and his plantigrade feet, account for that mincing gait characteristic of him. His fur is long, thick, and glossy black variegated with pure white. The white runs in a narrow stripe up the nose, expands behind the ears into a saddle-like patch on the nape of the neck, then narrows backward over the shoulder, and there divides, a stripe curving backward and downward on each side, leaving an intensely black, wedge-shaped tract between them, continued over the upper surface of the bushy tail. The under surface and tip of the tail are also white. This is the common Northern kind. His

Southern relatives are also black and white, but differently marked. All the skunks form a conspicuous exception to the prevalent rule among mammals that those parts of the body next the ground are light, the belly and limbs here being invariably dark colored. Thoreau pictures the animal neatly in a June memorandum:

" Saw a little skunk coming up the river bank in the woods at the white oak, a funny little fellow, about six inches long and nearly as broad. It faced me and actually compelled me to retreat before it for five minutes. Perhaps I was between it and its hole. Its broad black tail, tipped with white, was erect like a kitten's. It had what looked like a broad white band drawn tight across its forehead or top-head, from which two lines of white ran down, one on each side of its back, and there was a narrow white line down its snout. It raised its back, sometimes ran a few feet forward, sometimes backward, and repeatedly turned its tail to me, prepared to discharge its fluid, like the old ones. Such was its instinct, and all the while it kept up a fine grunting like a little pig or a red squirrel."

This resemblance to a fluffy-tailed black and white kitten has played the mischief with many kind-hearted but unsophisticated persons, — a reactionary sort of mimicry that it would puzzle Darwinians to explain, I fear. As a matter of fact, these youngsters are much more to be dreaded

than an old skunk, who will not waste his precious
ammunition until he has exhausted every "bluff"
he can practise.

This composure in the presence of mankind,
from whom nearly all wild animals shrink and flee,
has always been ascribed to the creature's confidence in his means of self-defence, which grows
upon him with experience, and inculcates a temerity in the face of danger that often misleads to
his destruction. Even in the skunk discretion is
usually the better part of valor : as it certainly is as
opposed to him. Whether or not the explanation
is good, he is certainly fearless and often serene
in the midst of danger ; he will not trouble himself to move out of the way of a wagon fast enough
to save being run over ; and half the time will
come inquisitively toward you, when you meet him,
instead of running away.

One effect of this audacity has been the tendency of skunks to cultivate acquaintance with
humanity as fast as the country was settled, — in
fact, before that, for they haunted Indian camps,
no doubt, in the primitive East as they do to-day in
the far West. Originally they possessed the whole
of temperate North America, reached northward
as far as the Barren Grounds in the interior, and
in Alaska to the lower Yukon valley ; while southward they penetrated Mexico, although that unhappy country and its neighboring parts of the
United States have several smaller, but sufficiently

effective, species of their own. As to details he is indifferent, — forest or prairie, open plain or rugged mountain, seeming all the same to his catholic taste in geography. If he exercises any preference, it is for high, dry, rocky situations for his particular residence, as opposed to waterside haunts chosen by his cousin the mink; in this respect he inclines more to the ways of the badger, to which he is so closely allied. Almost every-where, moreover, he is seen in greater numbers around settlements and camps than in the utter wilderness; and there are few rural districts where this animal is probably not quite as numerous to-day as he was a century or two centuries ago.

It is equally indifferent to climate. The snows of the North, the rainy districts of Puget Sound, the Atlantic coast and Alaska, the aridity of the high plains, are borne with equal patience; and everywhere it is resident. It never runs away from bad weather, any more than from sentient enemies. In the far North, it hibernates several months; on the Canadian border, this hiemal slumber lasts only for some weeks, with more or less frequent emergences during intervals of moderation; in the central and southerly parts of the United States, it does not "hole up" at all. The Canadian Indians called March the "skunk moon," because then the animal began to appear in some numbers, as they knew by the frequency of his diagonally placed footprints

in the snow, — the feet stepping at equal dis-
tances apart and in advance, — thus :

* * * * * *

 * * * * *

Dwelling under such varied conditions, it is
not surprising to find it making its home in a
variety of tenements. Its fore feet are armed
with long and strong claws, so that it is able
to dig well, and it habitually excavates burrows
in light soil. On the prairies, as Kennicott ascer-
tained, they are five to ten feet long and a foot
or so below the surface; but sizes vary. At the
innermost end is hollowed out a chamber well
bedded with grass. In the high Western mountains and other rocky places, it usually takes
possession of a crevice; and hollow trees and
stumps are now and then adopted as homesteads.
Burroughs says it appropriates woodchuck-holes
in New York State; and, in New England, stone
walls often form part, at least, of the shelter
needed for its den. Lastly, it has adopted everywhere the uncomfortable habit of seeking a lodging beneath the houses and barns of farmers and
ranchmen, making its presence known sooner or
later during the winter by a stench that compels
the landlord to evict the intruder straightway.

 Dr. Elliott Coues avers that this stench is the
result of the necessity the animal feels to evacu-
ate his scent-glands from time to time, when they
are not emptied by some provoked discharge, and

that the hibernating animal is occasionally aroused
from his torpidity to relieve his physical uneasiness
in this respect. Dr. C. C. Abbott agrees with him
as to the necessity of occasional relief, but says
that a series of observations in 1872 led him to
believe that this forced discharge was made by the
skunk into a hole dug for the purpose, where it
was carefully covered over. This strikes me as a
credible, and, indeed, very natural example of pru-
dence on the part of the animal (which must fully
understand what an advertisement of its presence
to its enemies the effluvium would be), closely comparable with the covering of its excrement prac-
tised by so many wild animals, — an act doubtless
precautionary against pursuit. In winter, however,
the frozen ground would prevent doing this, or, at
any rate, prevent doing it well. Certainly skunk
dens are rarely any more offensive to the nose than
is the home of a weasel or marten.

He is a persistent digger, and delights to scratch
holes in ploughed fields, where, if he is alarmed, he
will bury himself out of sight with amazing rapidity, and then may push his way through the light
earth for several yards before he comes to the surface again. Another cunning trick he has, when
trying to escape from a dog that is not right at his
heels, is to climb upon a rail fence and walk along
its top for a considerable distance, so as to break
the scent of his trail; but any further climbing
than this seems beyond his ability, so that the

picture illustrating, otherwise admirably, the biography of our subject in the ninth edition of the "Encyclopædia Britannica," where two examples are shown in the tops of tall trees, is something to smile at.

In the burrow or other den, where a large bed of grass and leaves is arranged, a litter of six to ten young ones is produced in summer. These remain in and about the underground premises until the next season, and by the end of the winter most of them have grown to the same size and appearance as the old ones. It was probably the digging out of single large and well-grown families supposed to be collections of unrelated adult individuals, that give rise to the wrong statement found in many early writings that the species is gregarious. They seem to be more prolific than any other of the Mustelidæ.

Young skunks, when taken early, make pretty and interesting pets. This was learned from the Indians, and they have been tamed and enjoyed by many persons notwithstanding, as Godman puts it, that "such a pet requires very cautious management." No one has had so much experience, or has so well recorded it, in this direction, as Dr. Merriam, whose home was formerly in the southern Adirondacks, where he made good use of many opportunities to study this creature. He declares that as pets skunks are attractive in appearance, gentle, cleanly, playful, and sometimes manifest considerable affection for those who have the care of them.   He says :

" From some I removed the scent-bags, but the greater number were left in a state of nature. None ever emitted any odor, although a couple of them, when half-grown, used to assume a painfully suggestive attitude on the too near approach of strangers. . . .   These same skunks, when I came within reach, would climb up my legs and get into my arms.   They liked to be caressed and never offered to bite."

One particularly clever youngster the Doctor named Meph, and used to carry asleep in his coat-pocket while driving about the country on his daily professional errands.   "After supper," he writes,[1] "I commonly took a walk, and he always followed, close at my heels.   If I chanced to walk too fast for him, he would scold and stamp with his fore feet, and if I persisted in keeping too far ahead would turn about, disgusted, and make off in an opposite direction; but if I stopped and called him, he would hurry along at a sort of ambling pace, and soon overtake me.   He was particularly fond of ladies, and I think it was the dress that attracted him; but be this as it may, he would invariably leave me to follow any lady that chanced to come near.

" We used to walk through the woods to a large

[1] In the Transactions of the Linnean Society of New York, Vol. I, December, 1882, p. 74.

meadow that abounded in grasshoppers. Here
Meph would fairly revel in his favorite food, and
it was rich sport to watch his manœuvres. When
a grasshopper jumped he jumped, and I have seen
him with as many as three in his mouth, and two
under his fore paws, at one time! He would eat
so many that his over-distended little belly actually
dragged upon the ground, and when so full that
he could hold no more, would still catch and slay
them. When so small that he could scarcely tod-
dle about he never hesitated to tackle the large
and powerful beetle known as the 'horned bug,'
and got many smart nips for his audacity. But
he was a courageous little fellow, and it was not
long before he learned to handle them with im-
punity, and it was very amusing to see him kill
one. Ere many weeks he ventured to attack a
mouse, and the ferocity displayed in its destruction was truly astonishing. He devoured the entire body of his victim, and growled and stamped
his feet if any one came near before his repast was
over."

This matter of growling and stamping is worth
a moment's attention. Few animals are so silent
as the skunk. Zoölogical works contain no information as to its voice, and the essayists rarely
mention it except by implication. Mr. Burroughs
says: "The most silent creature known to me, he
makes no sound, so far as I have observed, save
a diffuse, impatient noise, like that produced by

Q

beating your hand with a whisk-broom, when the farm-dog has discovered his retreat in the stone fence." Rowland Robinson tells us that: "The voiceless creature sometimes . . . frightens the belated farm-boy, whom he curiously follows with a mysterious hollow beating of his feet upon the ground." Thoreau, as has been mentioned, heard one keep up a " fine grunting, like a little pig or a squirrel "; but he seems to have misunderstood altogether a singular loud patting sound heard repeatedly on the frozen ground under the wall, which he also listened to, for he thought it "had to do with getting its food, patting the earth to get the insects or worms." Probably he would have omitted this guess if he could have edited his diary instead of leaving that to be done after his death. The patting is evidently merely a nervous sign of impatience or apprehension, similar to the well-known stamping with the hind feet indulged in by rabbits, — in this case probably a menace like a doubling of the fists, as the hind legs, with which they kick, are their only weapons. The skunk, then, is not voiceless, but its voice is weak and querulous, and it is rarely if ever heard except in the expression of anger. But I wish to quote a few more sentences from Dr. Merriam's story of his pet Meph:

" His nest was in a box at the foot of the stairs, and before he grew strong enough to climb out by himself he would, whenever he heard me coming,

stand on his hind legs with his paws resting on
the edge of the box, and beg to be carried up
stairs.   If I passed by without appearing to notice
him, he invariably became much enraged and chip-
pered and scolded away at a great rate, stamping,
meanwhile, most vehemently. . . .   He was very
sprightly and frolicsome, and used to hop about
the floor and run from room to room in search of
something to play with. . . .   During the evening
he occasionally assumed a cunning mood, and
would steal softly up to my chair, and standing
erect would claw at my pants once or twice, and
then scamper off as fast as his little legs could
carry him, evidently anxious to have me give
chase.   If I refused to follow, he was soon back,
ready to try some new scheme to attract my
attention."

The food of the skunks is wholly of animal origin, and I have never known or heard of one eating anything vegetable.   The staple of their fare
in summer is insects of every sort, mainly beetles,
grasshoppers, and the like, for they do not seem
to care to unearth worms and grubs to any great
extent.   Thoreau remarks (" Early Spring in Massachusetts," p. 105): "It has a remarkably long,
narrow, pointed head and [flesh-colored] snout,
which enable it to make those deep narrow holes
in the earth by which it probes for insects."   This
is news.   The snout is exceedingly pig-like — a
fact especially noticeable when a carcass has been

skinned, and it is no doubt serviceable in rooting, and in crowding through the loose earth in which the animal sometimes hastily buries itself ; but that it is used for rooting or boring, woodcock-fashion, after subterranean insects, I am not otherwise informed. The number of insects a single one will destroy, between his appetite and his love of play, is enormous ; and almost every one of them is injurious to grain, vegetable, or fruit crops. Of so much value to the hop-grower in particular are his services, that efforts were made some years ago in New York State to have him brought under protection of the game-laws. The facts brought forward then (and since) show that his value in ridding fields, gardens, and granaries of vermin compensated, a hundred times over, the occasional harm he does in the poultry-yard; but the prejudices of short-sighted farmers and the opposition of the fur-trappers defeated this beneficent measure.

Next to insects he probably pursues mice with the greatest avidity and success. The enormous destruction of planted seeds, growing and ripening vegetables and grain, as well as of stored grain, accomplished by wild mice, in all parts of the country, is well known to agriculturists, who ought to welcome, rather than do their best to extirpate, the natural enemies of these persistent and rapidly multiplying pests. The mice alone do more damage to the grain and fruit growing interests of

every agricultural district in the Union, each year,
than all the chickens and eggs raised therein are
worth. Yet men go on shooting and trapping
their would-be allies, and thus aiding and abetting
their enemies, in spite of all the facts and advice
that can be laid before them.

Unable, like the swift and supple weasel, to run
mice down or follow them into narrow retreats, —
though doubtless he pounces upon many, — the
skunk uses his strong fore claws to dig them out
of their little burrows and grassy lodging-places;
and it is the search for this prey, mainly, that leads
him to take up his quarters in the barns and outhouses of a farm, where he often inhabits the hay-
mow, scrambling even to the top of it. Unless disturbed to the point of odorous resistance by the
dogs — oh, that American farmers would kill off
the host of curs that do so much to keep them
poor! — his presence would scarcely be known,
or if discovered would not be resented; and hundreds, perhaps thousands, of mice would be killed
or driven away in the course of a season. The
same service is true to a less degree in the West,
by reason of its capture of the destructive striped
gophers and small prairie spermophiles there,
while even rabbits are now and then followed and
attacked, sometimes after following their trail a
long distance. These timid animals have a habit
of running into any sort of a hole, and frequently
enter one at the other end of which dwells a skunk,

fox, or badger, which makes short work of poor
bunny, and, I hope, is properly grateful to the
providence that thus sends a meal home in its
original package.

Reptiles, also, form a share of the skunk's subsistence, — toads, frogs, salmanders, serpents, and
the like.   Dr. Abbott says that the skunks in New
Jersey are very partial to the last-named.   "When
pressed by hunger, and hunting by daylight," he
tells us, in his "Rambles about Home," the skunk
prefers to go after snakes rather than to seek
frogs or risk himself within the poultry-yard.

"Indeed, small snakes are evidently a great
dainty, and the skunk appears to be more active
when he finds a garter-snake, blind-worm, or flat-
head adder, than at any other time.   Having discovered a snake, he rises upon his hind feet, and,
giving a bear-like apology for a dance, he endeavors to seize the snake by the tail.   If successful,
he shakes the snake vigorously, as a dog would do,
and seizing it, when dead or nearly so, he carries
it off to his burrow, or to a hollow log, or to whatever shelter he has at the time."

Of this behavior Dr. Abbott cites the following
remarkable instance :

"In June, 1863, I witnessed a terrific combat between a large skunk and a black snake, which, I
judge, measured fully five feet in length.   The
prowling skunk had evidently seized the snake by
the tail, and endeavored to give it a violent shake,

as it would a little garter-snake. This angered the
snake, and, turning like lightning, he wrapped
himself about the skunk, completely encircling
both neck and body. The head was so far free
that the skunk could give the snake nip after nip,
though it could not get a strong enough hold to
disable it. Rolling over and over, hissing and
snapping, the snake nearly concealed by the long
hair of the skunk, the two creatures presented a
strange spectacle as they struggled, the one to
conquer, the other to escape. After watching
them for fully five minutes, I ventured to approach,
and dealt the two a hard blow with a club, and
then ran back a few paces, not knowing what
might be the result. Turning about, I ventured
to return part of the way, to see whether the
struggle continued. All was comparatively quiet,
and coming still nearer, I found that the snake had
relinquished his hold, and was slowly retiring in
a disabled condition. The skunk was lying quite
motionless, and proved to be dying, though not
dead. Soon after, I examined the animal carefully,
and found that it had been strangled or nearly so.
During this combat there was no discharge of the
defensive glands of the skunk."

Unfortunately the skunk has also a strong taste
for birds and birds' eggs, and undoubtedly destroys large numbers of the eggs and young of
ground-nesting birds : it digs up and eats snakes'
and tortoises' eggs. Dr. J. K. Lord, whose book

"The Naturalist in British Columbia" is everywhere interesting, has harsher words to say of the skunk in that part of the world than the animal seems to justify elsewhere; but this may be discounted by the recollection that more legitimate food is rather scarce along the western part of the international boundary, where Dr. Lord travelled. "A more predatory, thievish, treacherous, bloodthirsty poacher you could not 'skeer up,'" exclaims this writer, and then adds novel information, as follows: "His residence (which is always by the side of some still pool on the open prairie) consists of a large hole, dug in horizontally. . . . Beaten roads extend from this hole to the water's edge; and the entrance to this den is usually strewed with ducks' feathers, the tips of the wings, the heads, beaks, and feet, together with bones deftly picked. Ducks are his favorite food. . . . When everything is still and hushed, and the unsuspecting birds are floating in fancied security, with their heads tucked under their wings, then out steals the crafty skunk, and creeping noiselessly down his roadways, swims, without the slightest splash, towards the drowsy birds, dives under the one that suits his taste, seizes it by the breast, and spite of all its flapping, quacking, and struggling, drags the victim ashore, kills, and eats it."

With such a record as this against him — even in isolated cases — it is not surprising that the skunk should now and then play havoc in the hen-

house. " He is a confirmed epicure, and at plun-
dering hen-roosts an expert," John Burroughs declares with an unction born of bitter experience :
" Not the full-grown fowls are his victims, but
the youngest, most tender. At night Mother Hen
receives under her maternal wings a dozen newly
hatched chickens, and with much pride and satis-
faction feels them all safely tucked away in her
feathers. In the morning she is walking about
disconsolately, attended by only two or three.
What has happened ? Where are they gone ?
That pickpocket, Sir Mephitis, could solve the
mystery. Quietly has he approached, under cover
of darkness, and, one by one, relieved her of her
precious charge. Look closely, and you will see
their little yellow legs and beaks or a part of a
mangled form lying about on the ground. Or,
before the hen has hatched, he may find her out,
and, by the same sleight of hand, remove every
egg."

This is sad ; but I am inclined to think both Dr.
Lord and Mr. Burroughs have let fancy run away
with them, and that such delicate knavery is more
often to be credited to the artistic touch of the
mink or weasel. The skunk is no fool, and may
perhaps be cunning enough, but he is too careless
and bull-headed to do his work with the neatness
and precaution against detection implied in the
operations described above. He goes boldly into
the roosting flock at night and slashes about him

with the carelessness of a Musketeer of the Guard;
and when the commotion brings the farmer and
his gun, it is ten to one whether he make a single
intelligent effort to get away.   As a matter of fact,
roost-robbery is only an occasional wickedness;
or, more truly, perhaps, it is only a few skunks who
adopt the habit of raiding the poultry-yard, and the
total of his depredations does not amount to a tithe
of the return he makes by his nocturnal activity
among the gophers, mice, and injurious insects.
Moreover, he has to bear the blame of most of
the misdeeds of the more stealthy and sagacious
fox, marten, and weasel.

What are the skunk's natural enemies?   Well,
like other of the smaller mammals, he must suffer
from the attacks of the larger ones, though it is
customary to assert — but this is largely an assump-
tion open to dispute — that he is not so frequently
seized as would be another animal equally tooth-
some and incautious, by the puma, wild-cats, wolves,
and large hawks and owls, all of which do sometimes kill and eat him.   He must now and then
get into fatal quarrels with the fox, badger, fisher,
mink, and other weasels with which he comes into
competition and contact, but against which he can
make a pretty nearly equal fight, regardless of his
quick-firing battery.

This suggests some interesting speculations as
to the actual value to the animal of its peculiar
defensive armature.   One would think, — consider-

ing its ability to adapt itself to any kind of country
or climate, as is shown by its almost continental
range; recalling the wide variety and plenty of
its food, not to speak of its faculty for avoiding
winter scarcity by sleeping its want away; and remembering the character of its anal artillery, —
one would think, I say, that, leaving humanity out
of the question, this animal had practically no limit
to its increase and longevity; and when one adds
to this the fact of its unusual prolificacy, it is surprising that the land is not positively overrun with
skunks.   Yet there never seems to have been any
disproportionate abundance of them.   One important check to their multiplication may be fatal intestinal parasites, derived from their prey, but these
are probably no more injurious to this carnivore
than to many others; and the wonder grows, —
not that there are so many skunks, but that there
are not millions more.

If Mr. Wallace and his friends are right, the
conspicuous coloring of the skunk is designed
(in a Darwinian sense) as a "warning" to all
and sundry in the forest to keep their distance.
On the back of every Northern skunk are bold
white bands and patches alternating with coal-
black, making it an object visible and attractive
to brute curiosity from a long distance; but, as
if to increase this notoriety to its utmost, the
animal always hoists its tail, and the tip of it
— or, in some species, the whole of this pompon-

like appendage — is glaring white. Conspicuous?
You can see it bobbing along above the grass
as far away as you can see anything of its size,
and know that "one o' thim pesky skoonks" is
wandering through the meadow when his body
is entirely concealed. So strong an example as
this has been quickly seized upon, of course, by
the Darwinians as an example of the effect of
natural selection in automatically producing serviceable colors; but perhaps the display does
not prove as useful to the skunk's welfare as
some less striking pattern would be. In his
highly interesting little book on Nicaragua, for
example, Belt remarks that "at night the skunk
goes leisurely along, holding up his white tail
as a danger-flag for none to come within range
of his dangerous artillery"; and adds: "The
animal is not likely to be pounced upon by any
of the carnivora mistaking it for other night-
roaming animals."

As a matter of fact, however, is it not "pounced
upon" quite as often as are other night-rovers?
I do not recall at the moment a record of a
puma having actually been known to have killed
a skunk, but there is no reason to suppose this
animal or the lynx or common wild-cat would hesitate to strike one down if he were hungry, — as
when is he not? The stealthy approach, sudden
spring, and back-crushing bite of one of these or
any other big cat would be a method of attack

that in most cases would give the artillerist no
opportunity to wheel into "action front"; and,
furthermore, it appears that when a close and
sudden combat occurs, as in the tussle with the
snake witnessed by Dr. Abbott, or such a fight
over spoil and right of way as would occur in
a burrow between two rival skunks or a com-
peting mink or badger, — a regular teeth-and-toe-
nail scrimmage, — the anal glands are not dis-
charged. A similar restraint would, no doubt, in
most cases attend the fierce and sudden swoop
of an owl, hawk, or eagle, — birds that cause the
death of many a skunk and conepate. If, as is
true, a comparatively slight blow across the small
of the back will paralyze and render powerless
the whole hind quarters of the animal, including
the gland-muscles, the deadly clutch of a heavy
bird's talons are likely to have a similar effect.
If the skunk has not judgment enough to let a
big black snake alone, as we have seen, probably
he must often (especially in the West) tackle a
rattlesnake or copperhead, whose prompt turn
and poisonous stroke could hardly be prevented
by any discharge of the glandular liquid.

(This suggests a parenthetical note to show how
these two creatures must sometimes encounter one
another under undesired circumstances. The rattling of the crotalus is wonderfully similar to that
of a grasshopper, — the skunk's favorite tidbit;
and that animal may occasionally be deceived into

running heedlessly upon a rattlesnake when it
expected to pounce upon a grasshopper.   A fight
might ensue, and both parties might be fatally
injured before explanations could be given ; but a
victory would be of no value to the reptile, at least,
for no rattlesnake could get even a half-grown
skunk down its throat.   In such a situation as
this the alleged "warning rattle" of the snake
would become a means of attraction instead of
repulsion, — of harm rather than benefit.)

There remain to be considered only foxes and
wolves as natural enemies of the skunk, other than
men and their dogs ; and as these alone attack
him boldly or by chase, in such a way as ordinarily
to inform him of danger in time to defend himself, it is against them mainly that his peculiar
weapon would be of service.   Now the fox is so
knowing, so sly and sagacious, that he must be
fully aware of what to expect, and take such pre-
cautions against harm to himself as distinguish
him elsewhere.   He has the nature of a dog, but
he has learned the strategy of the cat, and we are
bound to believe, from what we know of his cunning methods in respect to other prey, that he
takes good care to get the skunk at a disadvantage
before he attacks it.   Evidence of this is afforded
by the experience of trappers.   "To the fox-
trapper," says one intelligent writer on the subject,
"this animal is a pest, so that most of the skunks
of the neighborhood must be caught or got rid of

before success with the foxes begins. A slight
compensation is made by the fact that the taint
left about the setting-place attracts more foxes;
and trappers know that skunk-flesh is their best
bait. Sometimes when a skunk has been caught
by the foot he will free himself by self-amputation.
In such cases "they seldom get in a second time,
as in their weak and mutilated condition they fall
an easy prey to the fox, who is fond of their flesh:
so much so that he will sometimes gnaw off the
leg by which the skunk is held in the trap, and
carry off his booty to be eaten at leisure."

The wolf, on the other hand, from indifference
to caution, blind ferocity, and pure courage, seems
to take no such care. He knows he can easily
run down this slow-footed animal, and simply rushes
at him with open jaws. If, as usually happens,
no doubt, he gets a blast which burns his eyes and
mouth, and stifles him for the moment, he may
halt, but, maddened with pain and rage, will rush
again at the little animal the instant he recovers
vision and breath, and make mince-meat of it in
half a minute.

That this picture of the behavior of the wolf is
substantially accurate is shown not only by what
we actually know of both the gray wolf and coyote,
but by the behavior of dogs, any of which that
have any *hunt* in them, will dash at a skunk with
the utmost fury, whenever they get a chance, and
without an instant's hesitation. If the little beast

sees them coming, he prepares to fire, and never fails to hit his mark. "The instant a dog has received a discharge of this kind on his nose and eyes, he appears half distracted, plunging his nose into the earth, rubbing the sides of his face on the leaves and grass, and rolling in every direction." So says Audubon; and that skunk often goes free. But this authority adds that the same dogs do not hesitate to attack other skunks as soon after as they are able, and this despite severe punishments by their masters. Many other experiences to the same purport might be quoted, — for example, the dog of Mr. Fred Mather, long a Fish Commissioner of New York, which, driven back in his first attack, recovered spirit enough in a few minutes to rush in with streaming eyes and demolish the enemy; and which ever afterward killed skunks *with his eyes shut!*

As far as the mere stench is concerned, I doubt whether that deters any animals from attacking or consuming this or any other of the many animals noxious to *us* by reason of their musky secretions. We must be careful not to impute to the dogs, wolves, etc., the mental or physical disgust we feel at this vile odor. The fluid itself burns their eyes, nostrils, and throats, but the smell is more likely to attract than offend them; and it is probably the instinctive appreciation of this which leads the skunk to take the greatest care, by hoisting its tail and spreading its haunches, to prevent a

drop falling upon its own fur. Sometimes the
wind blows the liquid back; but the animal never
soils itself or its companions or its bed if it can
avoid it. A skunk's den is as nearly odorless as
is that of any wild musteline animal. Moreover,
it seems to regard the secretion as exceedingly
precious, and not to be used except as a very last
resort. Many a dog gets a good grip before the
emission occurs, and under those circumstances
it is likely to be quite wasted. "When caught in
steel traps," says Merriam, "not more than one in
twenty will smell, and the remaining nineteen
suffer themselves to be tormented to an astonishing degree before 'opening the valve.'" Men
who make a business of trapping and breeding
skunks seem to have little fear of them so long
as they approach them quietly and handle them
gently, and they know many ways of putting them
to death without causing a discharge.

It seems to me, therefore, that as a weapon of
defence the discharge of the skunk is not as
unfailing and complete as has been supposed;
that as many active enemies seek to kill the
animal, and probably succeed in killing it, as if it
did not have such a weapon; that, on the other
hand, it sometimes serves as an advertisement of
its presence and leads to its discovery by enemies
that might otherwise overlook it; that in resisting
the tactics of certain antagonists this "weapon"
is, as a rule, practically useless, since they keep

R

out of range, and in respect to others is inadequate, since it often causes only a temporary check (which the animal is too slow to take great advantage of), or does not stop the onslaught of all; lastly, it appears that the animal is loth to make use of the "weapon," and often delays doing so until it is too late. It remains a question, therefore, whether the possession of this ability is not a disadvantage rather than a help to the animal; and whether in the process of development the influences of natural selection have not freed the other Mustelidæ from it, as an incumbrance, rather than have developed it to a high degree in this species as an advantageous accessory.

As to his conspicuous colors and ostentatious manner of cocking up his white plume of a tail, these seem to be a "warning" only to civilized man, and even to him a signal that leads more often than otherwise to the animal's premature discovery and death; while, if the statements above written are true, this indiscreet display of himself only shows the big cats, the wolves, birds of prey, and the farmer's dog, where their quarry is, and enables them to plan an attack before they themselves have been observed.

The skunk is coming to be considered more and more valuable as a fur-bearer; and his coat, cleansed of any possible odor, dyed a uniform black, and made up into garments, clothes many a fair maid who is told she wears "Alaska sable."

It is sable only in artificial hue, and probably came
from Connecticut; but it is a good, warm, handsome fur for all that, and there is no occasion to
gird at its real origin.   It seems to me that the
use of the skins without dyeing, employing their
natural contrast of white and black, might serve
admirably in certain goods, as robes; but this is
rarely if ever seen.   If the reason is that the prej-
udice against the name is too great to be overcome with the average purchaser, several better
euphemisms than the false and meaningless
"Alaska sable" might have been chosen by the
furriers.   Nobody knows the source of the word
skunk, but it is probably an early Canadian French-
English shortening and corruption of the Abenaki
Indian term *secancu* or the Huron *scangaresse*.
The Crees of the Canadian Northwest called the
animal *seecawk*; but a better trade name would
have been *chinga*, by which the animal became
known to the early European naturalists by specimens from French sources in the Mississippi
valley.

The pelts are now worth from fifty cents to one
dollar and a half to the trapper.   The business at
best is not one calculated to make the practitioner
popular in fastidious society; and reminds one of
the force of the somewhat coarse maxim formerly
quoted in admonishing a person not to spread
abroad home-scandals, — "Let every man skin
his own skunk!"

The oil procured by boiling the bodies of skunks is also a commodity salable to druggists, and worth at present about fifty cents a pound to the maker. The demand has increased of late, the oil (applied externally) having high repute as a relieving agent in diseases of the chest and bronchial tubes, especially croup, for which it has been a household remedy in New England since Colonial days. There is no reason to suppose, however, that it has any medicinal value different from or superior to any other fine animal oil, which easily penetrates the pores and mollifies and lubricates the air-passages; its supposed special efficacy in bronchial disorders is doubtless a superstitious transference to the oil of the unquestioned value in some phases of such disorders of the substance of the scent-glands, — a remedy based upon entirely different qualities and effects than are possessed by this oil, or that of the rattlesnake or any other out-of-the-way creature, highly regarded in "old-woman" doctoring. When relief follows an application it may be considered a faith-cure, in so far as any particular effect of this specific kind of oil is concerned.

However this may be, there is a steady demand for the commodity; and as a fat skunk will yield a pound and a half, there is profit in making it. Thus the systematic catching of skunks has become a regular business in certain regions, where they are plentiful, and many persons are engaged in it, particularly in Connecticut, New York, and Penn-

sylvania.   In several localities, in fact, large en-
closures have been set apart for the breeding and
rearing of these animals for profit, such places
being known as "skunkeries." No animal is more
easily trapped.   He seems to be stupid beyond
belief in this respect, and will walk into a deadfall,
or step into a spring-trap or get himself caught in
almost any simple device that most animals would
simply laugh at.   One favorite trick is to climb
into a barrel that he knows or fancies contains
something good to eat, without heeding that he
cannot climb out again.   Merriam says that a
steel trap, set at the mouth of an inhabited burrow
will often capture the entire family at the rate of
one a night.   "In winter half a dozen or more
may sometimes be taken in a single night, in the
following manner : the hunter treads a narrow
path in the snow, leading from the mouth of the
hole away in the direction of some favorite resort,
and, at intervals along this path, the traps are set
in the snow.   At nightfall, when the skunks come
out, they march, single file, down the path, the
mother usually taking the lead.   The head one is
generally caught in the first trap, and the others
climb over the resulting obstruction, and move on
till a second is taken, and a third, and so on."

The flesh is edible.   Not only were the Indians
everywhere fond of it, but most white men, who
have been able to forget the associations of the
name, agree that the flesh is white, tender, juicy,

and as good as suckling-pig, which it resembles. This of course implies that the animal has been carefully skinned and freed from its glands. The *voyageurs* of the Northwest were accustomed to skin and dissect the animal under running water, which rid it of its skunkiness; in Nova Scotia, at the other end of the continent, the Indians ate it without minding whether it was tainted or not, according to Gilpin.

One topic in connection with this subject might be debated at length here, did it seem worth while; namely, the exhibition of rabies in the skunk, communicating hydrophobia to any human being bitten by an affected animal. Very full discussion of this may be found in the "American Journal of Science and Art"[1] for May, 1874, by the Rev. H. C. Hovey; and this has been extensively quoted and commented upon by Dr. Elliott Coues in his "Fur-Bearing Animals," by William A. Baillie-Grohman in his "Camps in the Rockies," and by other competent authorities, so that the facts connected with the subject are accessible to most readers. In a word, the occasional appearance of rabies among skunks is a well-known fact in all parts of the country, and it has frequently happened that men and dogs bitten by these animals have subsequently died of hydrophobia. It has been alleged that this was a disease distinguished as mephitic

[1] Third series, Vol. VII, No. 41, Art. XLIV, pp. 477–483, May, 1874.

rabies, independent of canine rabies; while others assert that it is simply canine madness communicated to skunks by some mad dog, fox, or wolf, and thence started as a local epidemic among the skunks of the neighborhood. My own view inclines to the latter opinion. Certainly the bite of a skunk is ordinarily no more to be feared than that of any other wild animal, wounds from whose teeth are always liable to be followed by blood-poisoning due to particles of corrupt flesh adhering to the teeth and left in the wounds.

What has been said in all the foregoing pages applies to skunks in general, as a study of character, habits, and qualities, though more especially to the common Northern species known in zoölogy as *Mephitis mephitica.* In the southwestern United States and northern Mexico two other very similar species are distinguished, — *Mephitis macrura* and *M. estor.* In addition to this a closely allied group of skunks inhabits the warmer parts of the continent, known as the Little Striped Skunks, and constituting the genus Spilogale. These are decidedly smaller than Mephitis, and instead of the two more or less broad stripes reaching backward from the nape of the neck on each side of the spine (their shape and extent is very variable), four narrow and often broken and irregular white stripes lie upon the neck and shoulders, while the sides and rump are marked by transverse curving lines and spots; these lines are subject to great variation, and often are broken into spots and bars, which variegate the black pelt in a very handsome way. One of these little fellows (*Spilogale putorius*) is distributed throughout most of the Southern States and the whole region west of the Mississippi River. They can be domesticated like the others; and it is said that in Florida they are sometimes tamed and kept about the house, like cats, on account of their usefulness in catching mice. Several other species of Spilogale are found in the dry region stretching from Southern Utah to Central Mexico. Finally, we have, in Texas, and thence southward throughout Central and South America, the white-backed skunk, which the aborigines of Mexico called conepate, and naturalists call *Conepatus mapurito*. This species is rather larger than the common skunk, its head is narrower, and the snout more pig-like, and bald and callous on top, as if used to much rooting; while the tail, instead of being a long plume, is a short, stubby brush. In color it is black, like the others; but instead of stripes the whole back is white, from the forehead to and including the tail, giving a very striking blanket-like effect, but this often stops short of the tail, or is divided by a narrow black line along the spine. The next nearest relatives are the sand-badger and teledu of Southern Asia.

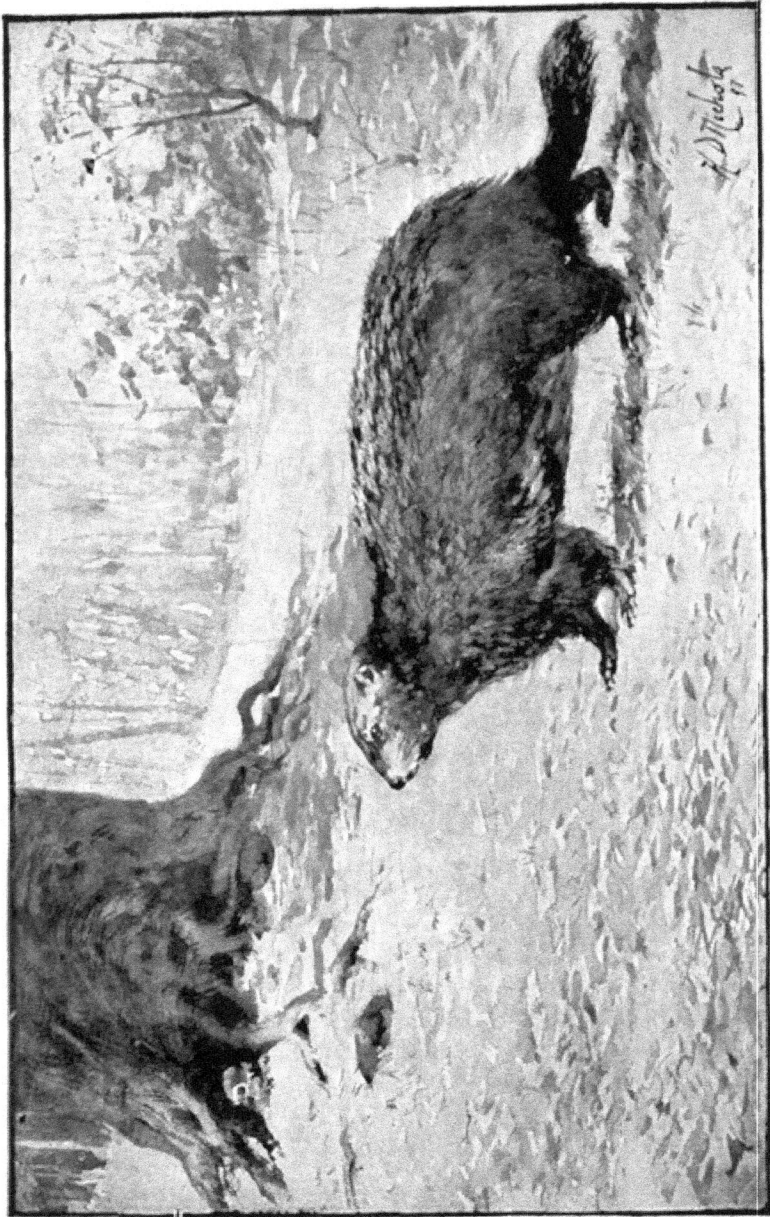

THE WOODCHUCK.

A NATURAL NEW ENGLANDER

WHETHER one considers the woodchuck in its relation to New England, or New England with reference to the woodchuck, the singular adaptability of each to the other is at once apparent. It is the foremost success and pride of the Yankee that he uses his means and material to the best advantage, — gets the utmost effect out of the least expenditure. It is the boast of the woodchuck that he has reduced the life of a quadruped in a northern climate to its lowest terms, and takes less trouble and worry, in the course of a fat and happy year, than any other beast of the field.

This is true, and he and the Yankee manage to thrive together, coming out about even when the books are annually balanced in October. Each reflects upon the other's qualities with growing respect, while separated by winter; and studies over the next move in the discussion of the question, "Who owns the clover-patch?" Then, some fine spring morning, the man finds only gnawed stubs in the place of certain succulent young vegetables he had selfishly saved for his

dinner, shakes his fist over the fence, muttering
"Durn that 'chuck!" whereupon the animal sits
up peart, as every independent New Englander
has a right to do, and whistles back: "Keep cool;
your old lettuce wasn't much good anyhow!"

Surely there are excellent reasons why the
animal should thrive and increase, in spite of
widening civilization, from the Housatonic to the
St. Croix, and from Lake Champlain to Cape Cod,
for not only the physical conditions, but the mental
and moral atmosphere, of New England suit him.
He approves of Yankee institutions, and does his
best to fall in with them and be pleasant about it.
It is therefore disheartening that he is often misunderstood.   He has broad views of hospitality,
for example, and it pains him to find himself
unwelcome in the farmer's garden, — positively in
peril of violence, sometimes, — when he himself
is entirely willing that his human neighbors should
visit his meadow and clover-field, and even carry
away as much of the crop as they like, since the
good Lord has sent enough for all.

Other slight misunderstandings exist; but, on
the whole, the two New Englanders differ more in
the number of their legs than in anything else, —
except, perhaps, in views as to the object of life,
which is not a matter for quarrelling between
friends.   Their aims are substantially the same, —
in a word, to get the most for the least; and, on
the whole, the four-legged one seems to have

attained to the higher success. The woodchuck manages, for instance, to shirk the tribulations of winter altogether, yet at the same time to stay where he is, and to stop all expenses. Whenever the Yankee tries to do that, he is obliged to undertake a toilsome journey and double his expenditures. But to comprehend the nature and appreciate the success of this admirable economist, we must acquaint ourselves with his ideals and methods.

The woodchuck is born in humble circumstances, as one of four or five equally young and poor, but honest, brothers and sisters. His natal chamber is a snug room, retired some three feet under ground, and his birthday is never far from the first of May. It is not only well for a little 'chuck to start with regularity upon his methodical career, but it prevents heartburning and strife to have all the youngsters in the community of practically the same age; it also facilitates their education, both for teachers and taught, when the whole body of youth can progress together from the kindergarten to commencement-day, and be graduated *en masse*. The concluding studies, no doubt, are practical instructions as to mining, courses upon the avoidance of projectiles, and tactics of warfare with dogs, with occasional lectures upon the mechanics of traps and the art of tree-climbing. Some of the more ambitious even emulate their human fellow citizens by going to

college, — as all the Wellesley girls of a few years
ago are able to testify, regularly joining in the
morning exercises with a clear soprano from the
chapel lawn.

Within a very few days the little ones are able
to stumble down the long hallway that leads to
their castle-door, and to open their brown eyes
upon a beautiful green world preparing to greet
the coming June. The breeze comes soft and
odorous to the fresh nostrils that snuff it up like
an elixir, shadows are trembling upon the emerald,
edible sward, and an infinitude of music salutes
the small ears that now for the first time may be
opened, since there is no longer danger of dust
falling into them. Clinging timorously to the
brown fur of the mother, they trot and tumble
after her, marvelling at everything, and halting in
wonder as with every few steps she rears herself
upon her haunches and gazes far and near over
the heads of the blossoming grass. Some even
try to imitate her, and, until they tumble backward,
sit up with head on one side and ears pricked,
pretending to listen most intently. By and by
they will learn to discriminate, among the confused
murmurs that tremble upon their ears, those that
threaten from those meaning no harm. The
farmer will tell you that no other animal has
hearing so acute, enabling it to perceive noises
that escape his notice altogether; yet their ears
are small, seem muffled in fur, and may be

pressed down, dust-tight, when the animal is tunnelling.

The young shoots of the grasses and weeds smell good, and the cubs exercise their white new teeth in nibbling these a little, but the mother guides them on further to a treat — a bunch of plantain ; and there they get their first out-door meal.   As they grow older they learn to like many different vegetables, but never lose their special fondness for the juicy plantain.

Day by day they develop in size, strength, and accomplishments.   As playful as other youngsters, they roll, and tumble, and chase one another, but never go so far away that they cannot scuttle back to the ancestral burrow the instant the warning whistle of some watchful companion tells them a boy, or dog, or other dreaded creature is coming. In the old days, before the Yankees took the trouble to "improve" a country that, in some respects at least, was better before they began, the woodchucks all lived in the woods —

" As their name implies," you say ?

Hold on a bit, my friend.   That word "wood-chuck" is bad English for a half-forgotten Indian term, and has nothing to do with "woods" at all. But let us go on.

And although often, doubtless, they sought the grassy glades and river-bottoms for food, they were not tenants of the open country, and were scarcely known on the Western prairies until emigrants settled there, planting clover-fields and garden-patches, when the woodchucks followed to see that everything was right, and that none of the good things should be wasted. They still make their winter homes more often in the woods, in all parts of the country, than in cleared ground.

Finding an abundance to eat, and being eager to fulfil their whole duty in that direction, the young ones grow rapidly, and carry their games farther and farther afield. Woodchucks do not dwell in companies, nor make "towns," like their Western cousins, the prairie-dogs; but it is never far to a neighbor's hole, visits back and forth soon become frequent, and the next thing one knows the youngsters are big and bold enough to go wandering off by themselves, seeking adventures and often finding them.

Now is the time—in these long midsummer days, when the hay is ripening and garden-sauce is at its best — when that old quarrel with the farmer begins, because he will not take their view of things. The woodchuck can no more see the propriety of fencing off — though he admits that stone walls are fine refuges, in case he has to run for it — a space of the very finest fodder, than the British peasant can see the right of shutting him out of a grove where there are wild rabbits, or forbidding him to fish in a certain stream. So he climbs over, or digs under, or creeps through, the fence, and makes a path or a playground for himself

amid the timothy and the clover, and laughs, as he
listens from a hole in the wall or under a stump,
to hear the farmer using language which is good
Saxon but bad morals, and the dog barking himself into a fit.   Next day he watches his chance,
invites his best friend to the feast, and makes his
way to a certain bed of lettuce, to a field of celery,
to rows of juicy beets and cabbages, or best of all,
to a patch of peas, — he will risk his whiskers for
green peas! — where the two rascals will stuff
their cheeks and fill themselves until their bulging
stomachs fairly drag upon the ground.   Then the
farmer swears harder than ever, and if the greedy
marauders try to repeat their performance, ten to
one they will get buckshot inside their ribs, or
find themselves prisoners in the torture of a trap.
Woodchucks seem never to "catch on " to a trap,
until it has caught on to them.

One, having thus, or otherwise, fallen into the
hands of a naturalist many years ago, was labelled
Arctomys monax, — the monk bear-mouse; and the
tribe has never been able to get rid of it.

Another unkindness, in woodchuck opinion, is
the way folks laugh at his gait and movements.
He feels no call to hurry, and he does not consider
it a just matter for ridicule that many other
animals are able to outrun him.   His ambitions
are intellectual rather than athletic.   If he is loose
in his clothes — well, so is man's favorite, the cat;
and he thinks it is unfair, when some one sees him

s

coming cautiously down a rock, to say that his
flabby body "pours itself over the ledge." His gait,
he asserts, is no more a waddle than that of the
ducks, in which farmers take so much delight. But
all this is only a part of the injustice with which he
feels that mankind regards his race. It does not
lead him to retaliate, being a hater of strife, but
only causes him to withdraw his society as much
as possible from those who will not treat him with
respect. None of us can escape criticism, and
vanity is universal, but life is too short to be
wasted in losing one's temper.

Most persons agree, however, that when our
little friend sits up on the tripod of his hind legs
and short, stiff tail, as he is fond of doing, and
eats his morsel like a gentleman or a squirrel, —
when you come to classify him you find him
nothing but a big ground-squirrel, after all, — the
woodchuck is an interesting fellow, and not in the
least ridiculous. His coat is soft reddish brown,
with a good deal of variety in it, from yellowish
gray to those Canadian ones that are almost black;
his nose, chin, and cheeks are gray or yellowish; his cap, tail, and feet are brownish black; while
his eyes are large and bright ; and when he pricks
up his ears and looks and listens with his head on
one side, and his hands drooped in fine-lady
fashion, there is a "cunning" aspect in his face
that makes you forgive him all his sins. Once in
a while a young one will rise up out of the brown

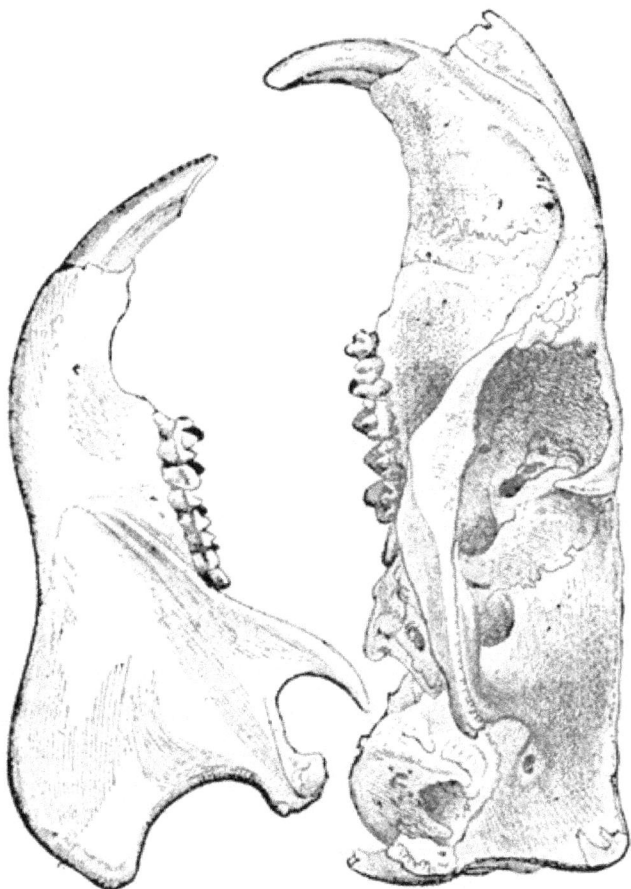

SKULL AND DENTITION OF A WOODCHUCK.—Natural size. After Baird.

leaves and look at you with eyes so full of surprised innocence that you haven't the heart to
scare him by even a loud word.

Sometimes folks insist upon a closer acquaintance, and, capturing a young one, take him into
the house. Then the woodchuck does his best to
please, and makes a delightful pet, cleanly, teachable, and not too much inclined to mischief.

But even a young woodchuck has to settle down
and be serious after a while; and his way is to
begin by falling in love. This is as easy as falling
off a log, and is not the serious part. I shall not
pry into the secrets of the rustic courtship, what
time the trembling swain invites his shy friend to
the summer-garden of mint and plantain at the
edge of the orchard; or when, surprised by canine
brigands, he gallantly pushes her behind him into
a cave or refuge beneath the old apple roots and,
facing the foe, clashes his teeth in fierce defiance
until the vagrom dogs retire; nor, least of all,
shall we follow the enamoured two as they steal
side by side across the midnight meadow, passing
from moonlight to shadow and back into moonlight again, as lovers must, parting the fragrant
blossoms, nibbling here a tidbit, and taking there a
sip of dew, then hurrying homeward as the golden
crescent hangs in the tree-tops, alarmed at the
lateness they had forgotten.

Now life begins as much in earnest as it is possible for a pair of woodchucks to know. This

brother and that have already gone thither and
yon to set up for themselves, some liking to stay
close to the ancestral burrow, others, having a roving
disposition, emigrating to the next farm, or even as
far as the further slope of the hill.   Mindful of the
parting advice of the old pair, — "Above all things
choose a place where a freshet or heavy rain will
not flood you out of house and home," — the young
couple take a sunny hillside long ago selected.   It
is crowned by rocky woods bounded by an old
stone wall, and thence slopes down in grassy pasture to the meadows and gardens along the river.
Many a deep hole — a sort of playhouse — has
the young husband dug when a boy, — you may
see New England pastures pitted with these bach-
elor experiments in tunnelling; but now he must
work steadily and for a purpose.   His feet are
armed with powerful claws, and the toes are partly
webbed, so that they make excellent shovels; and
when he encounters a bit of hard-packed earth, or
a stone, he has a pickaxe in his strong front teeth,
which quickly cuts down or loosens the obstacle.
Shovelling the dust beneath him, he now and then
stops and backs out, kicking vigorously, until he
has swept all the loose stuff to the entrance of the
tunnel, and has sent it flying outward.   First, he
slants steeply down for three or four feet, and
then begins to work upward (and here is the advantage of a hill-slope site), so that there will be
ready drainage away from his living room at the

inner extremity. He does not care much whether his tunnel is straight or curved. If he meets a rock or large root, he goes around it ; and he usually excavates two or three short branches, one of which is afterward used as a place for depositing all excrement and refuse. At last, twenty or twenty-five feet from the entrance, he stops, and scoops out a chamber big enough for the two of them to turn around in comfortably. This done, the young wife makes a basket of her cheeks, and carries in enough grass for a soft bed. Meanwhile her mate has extended a branch of the tunnel to the surface, opening there, beneath a tussock of grass or stump or stone, a small exit against a time of need, as when a mink, weasel, or big snake invades the premises ; but no hillock of earth is thrown out around this back door, to attract attention.

Such is the home of the old-fashioned contented woodchuck family ; but that admirable disposition in this race to steadfastly reduce exertion to a minimum, is leading the more thoughtful ones to get rid of the last vestige of the labor slavery of their ancestors, and release themselves from even housebuilding. Many young 'chucks, nowadays, therefore, simply renovate abandoned burrows of the year before, for it is the fashion in Arctomid society to change the dwelling-place annually ; or they seek a retreat in the hollow that nature has kindly opened for their accommodation beneath and within some ancient tree; or even take possession of a cavity in the stone wall that the farmer has thoughtfully provided. The Yankee calls this laziness. Here again the woodchuck protests that such a view is calumnious and unphilosophical. He declares that it is a wicked waste of time and energy to do anything avoidable not in the direct line of happiness, which, as every one knows, consists in gambolling among odorous herbage, swinging in the top of a bush, climbing trees, — a method of seeing the world every whit as good as laborious travel, — soaking for hours in the sunshine, strolling in the moonlight, and contemplating one's increase of fatness as autumn approaches. Why work when one may play? Why play when one may loaf? Why loaf when one may sleep? And the 'chuck further complains of the impropriety of harsh criticism from men who boast of their labor-saving machines, which, in his opinion, are labor-making, since they exist in order that two men shall work — but differently — where only one worked before.

"And yet," he goes on, as he sits up with his gray old back leaning comfortably against a smooth boulder, and chatters at me, with a burr in his speech and clattering teeth that make his words difficult to understand at first, —

"And yet they call it 'labor-saving,' and say that they are doing this ceaseless, prodigious struggling, in order to get a chance to rest and enjoy themselves. It's too deep for a woodchuck!

If they want to get rid of work, why in the world don't they stop working? Look at Hiram Coffin over there. When I was a little cub he lived in a log-cabin. I never could get up early enough to be ahead of him in the fields, and couldn't keep my eyes open late enough to see him go in. Still he sang and whistled (almost as good as a wood-chuck, sometimes), and now and then went on a spree, so that I concluded he was as happy as he knew how to be. Next year he put up an addition to his cabin and then had to work so hard to pay for it that he had no time to sing at all. Now" — pointing a black-gloved paw across the valley — " behold that big brick mansion he's building; and look at *him!* He's bent and stiff and thin. Thin? why, he wouldn't last through the winter in the best burrow on the hill! He has to wear tight boots and a close collar, and worries from morning till night for fear the bank will break, or bugs will get into his wheat, or his winter fires burn up his new house.

" Now look at me! In my first year I nearly wore myself out digging a long tunnel: some were good enough to say it was the finest burrow in the valley. Next year I cleaned out a hole left by a fool 'chuck that wanted to 'see the world,' and got nabbed by a dog — and served him right! Last year I wasted a beautiful day in enlarging a cave under a stump. This fall I have my eye on a hollow log, and my wife and I will stuff it with grass in half an hour, and sleep there just as happily as if it had cost a fortnight's digging."

It is too bad that such calm philosophers as this should be annoyed by dogs and hunters. Even Thoreau, finding a respectable woodchuck engaged in its doorway in conversation with some one inside, reached in, seized it by the tail, dragged it out, and flung it far down hill. Could any indignity be greater, or, from that source, more unexpected? Worse than this, some folks, having learned it from the aborigines, desire marmot skins for mittens, wallets, and the like; and even try to catch the poor things in order to eat their flesh.

That the animal is not really spiritless and lazy, but deliberately reposeful, is shown by the way that, when pursued, he can exert reserve energy to good purpose in getting into a place of safety; and having his means of retreat strategically secure, is willing and able to give valiant battle. Then the chattering and growling of his voice, and the clattering and gritting of his teeth, make any enemy think twice before proceeding to close quarters. This gives him time to rush to his castle, into which he plunges, flinging scorn and defiance at his impotent foes. If a ferret penetrates his defences, or a man digs them up, he steals from his postern gate and hurries to new intrenchments. Hence in the South, when a person is seen working with feverish energy at a hopeless task, men shake their heads and remark that it is a "ground-hog case," — that is, a useless proceeding.

When the meadows have been mowed, and from the stubble springs up a magnificent crop of clover, comes the heyday of the woodchuck's year. His midsummer housework is done, his mind is free from care, and he may eat all he wants of this daintiest of food. There is nothing he likes so well and nothing that does him so much good. His cheeks widen, his ribs are distended, and his loose skin is stretched out sleek with fatness. At last the 'chucks can hold no more, and need only loaf in the September warmth and doze away the time until the sun crosses the equinoctial line at the end of the month. This is the blessed date when etiquette permits them to refuse longer to tax themselves with social amenities, and to begin their Lenten fast.

One after another each pair of woodchucks retreat dozily to their beds, curl up side by side into two balls of warm fur, and fall fast asleep. A week later the most diligent searcher will not once hear the "chuckling diminuendo of the wood-chuck's whistle" of which Mr. Robinson speaks, for not a single *siffleur* is to be found on top of the ground. Warm sunny days may succeed one another, frost and snow may hold off for weeks, but the woodchuck pays no heed. His rule enjoins him to go to sleep by the first of October; therefore to sleep he goes, and stays there with that fixity of purpose that only the devotee of method can attain to. Even the pet in your house, kept warm the year through, will curl up in his kennel (or, better, in your cellar) and be indifferent to the world until his duty of sleep has been fulfilled. Pick him up, and you will think him dead, so rigid, cold, and insensible is he. Only the most delicate instruments show that his heart beats and that the blood still oozes sluggishly through his inert veins. He will survive for hours in a jar of carbonic-acid gas, where he would drown, when awake, in two minutes. It is true that you may carefully thaw him out, but the moment you let him alone he will drop into slumber again, regardless of temperature. And so his winter passes in one long dream of summer.

Could anything be sweeter or more convenient? Having only provided a shelter, he forthwith rids himself of winter. He need make no other preparation. Wrapped in his own fur, warmed and fed by the slow consumption of the fat which it was the supreme pleasure of his life to acquire, apathetic to cold, hunger, fear, or fretting, he escapes not only the famine and freezing to which such animals as are abroad all the year are exposed, but the hard work required of those, like the chipmunk, which must fill a storehouse in advance, in order to feed during the months of scarcity. Ah, he is a canny old marmot!

But, sad to say, few things in this world are

still quite perfect, and even the woodchuck's system of life has room for improvement.   As it
sends him to bed at the autumnal equinox, so it bids
him awake at the vernal equinox, and this is too
early in modern New England.   They say that he
often comes out even earlier, — some will tell you
on Candlemas Day, and others on St. Valentine's
Day (sometimes called Woodchuck Day by the
Yankees, who do not take much stock in foreign
saints); then he looks for his shadow, and if he
can see it he takes it as a sign that he would better
return to his bed.

> "The festive ground-hog wakes to-day,
>   And with reluctant roll
> He waddles up his sinuous way
>   And pops forth from his hole.
> He rubs his little blinking eyes
>   So heavy from long sleep,
> That he may read the tell-tale skies —
>   Which is it — wake or sleep?
>
> "And next he turns three times around,
>   For it is written so,
> That if his shadow 's on the ground
>   Or outlined in the snow,
> He fain must tumble in again,
>   For so tradition says,
> And snooze away down in his den
>   For forty more long days."

That is the way a poet of the newspaper-corner
expresses it; but I have never beheld such an

inquirer abroad, and am inclined to think the tale
an idle fancy : the woodchuck is too level-headed
to be likely to take counsel of a shadow.

He does certainly appear at the end of March,
however, even though, as usually happens, he
must bore his way out through a snow-bank.   He
is then weak and lean and hungry, and is likely to
starve before the fresh grass appears.

I am at a loss how to explain this defect in the
woodchuck's system (unless he is accounted a Jack-
sonian Democrat from the South, unwilling to con-
cede anything to Northern ideas, even of climate),
except by the theory that his conservatism has for
once led him into disadvantage.   There is such a
thing as the precession of the equinoxes, those cos-
mic dates upon which the marmot's whole reckon-
ing appears to be based ; these change a trifle every
year, and the effect in the course of time is to
bring the seasons and the names long ago applied
to them out of coincidence.   The woodchuck
family is a very ancient one, and highly connected ;
when it first knew the autumnal equinox by name,
the late frosts had killed the herbage, nights were
cold, and bed-time was truly at hand.   Similarly
in those days the vernal equinox really marked the
end of cold weather, the disappearance of snow,
and the sprouting of green leaves.   But while, with
a commendable clinging to ancient ways, the woodchucks have been faithfully following old traditions,
the rascally earth has been wabbling in its orbit

until the seasons have slipped back, and now the animal goes to sleep long before he need, and wakes up a month or two before he ought.

An astronomer tells me that there is much force in this theory, but points out a trifling difficulty in the fact that it is wrong end to, since the effect of the *precession* of the equinoxes is to advance, rather than retard, the *procession* of the seasons! You can study the matter out for yourself and welcome. The woodchucks have shown themselves otherwise possessed of so much clearheadedness and philosophic wisdom, that I expect soon to hear of their calling a council like that which reformed our human calendar, and setting this matter straight. That done, I see nothing left for the most captious woodchuck to desire, and the rest of us may then admire one bit of the world perfected!

X

A LITTLE BROTHER OF THE BEAR

THE raccoon is a truly American animal, even to its name. Captain John Smith, in his report upon Virginia, mentions "a beast they call Aroughcun, much like a badger, but vseth to liue on trees as Squirrels doe." The rapid Americans quickly shortened these sonorous syllables to "raccoon," with the emphasis thrown strongly on the last syllable, and now we usually cut even that down to *'coon.*

Truly if you were to dock his tail to a mere scut, and not compare the markings on his face too closely, he is "much like a badger" as the observant Smith said; but this is an accidental and outward likeness soon forgotten, for the sharp, flexible nose, the delicate, flat-soled feet, the arched hind quarters, and the long ringed tail quickly impress themselves upon a new acquaintance. You soon see that he is really a miniature Bruin — "that brief summary of a bear," as Burroughs styles him. In fact the early zoölogists simply put him in the genus Ursus, and had done with it; but closer examination of his anatomy, while

RACCOONS IN THE TREE-TOPS.

it left him in the bear family, gave him a separate genus, — Procyon. Our common Eastern raccoon is *Procyon lotor:* another belonging to Central and South America is *Procyon cancrivorus,* — the crab-eater.

According to Mr. J. A. Allen, a comparison of Northern with Southern specimens shows a gradual increase in size southward, amounting to a seventh or eighth of the bulk. There is also a tendency to an increase in the intensity of the colors in the same direction; and this anatomist considers that these variations explain away the "blackfooted," "psora," and two or three other nominal species formerly distinguished.

Its range extends throughout the wooded parts of the country as far northeast as central New Brunswick, and northwest into northern British Columbia, while it occurs sparingly on the North Saskatchewan.

The raccoon is one of the most thoroughly nocturnal of all our mammals; and he hibernates throughout the northern part of his range, more or less unbrokenly, according to the weather, so that only those know him well, in his wild condition, who are in the country at all seasons. Fortunately, however, he is easily trapped and makes a contented pet and convenient subject for study.

This simplicity of mind, which makes him unsuspicious of novelties, seems to show that he is not entitled to all of the reputation for acuteness

that has been given to him. Perhaps the fox is
his superior in real mental capacity, but the raccoon is so far beyond Reynard and many other
highly sagacious beasts in manual dexterity, that
he *appears* to be quite as clever as the best of
them. Add to this the remarkable acuteness of
his hearing, aided by sharp eyes and a quick nose,
and it is no wonder that "sly" has come to be
an accepted epithet describing him.

The 'coon most often makes his home in a hollow
tree, and is an excellent climber, yet he is not an
arboreal animal, in the sense that a squirrel is. As
Dr. Merriam puts it :

"They do not pursue their prey amongst the
tree-tops, after the manner of the martens ; nor
make a practice of gathering nuts from the
branches, like squirrels ; nor do they, like the
porcupine, browse upon the green foliage. Trees
constitute the homes in which they rest and bring
forth their young, and to which they retreat when
pursued by man or beast ; but their business is
transacted elsewhere."

The home of the raccoon family is usually in a
hollow high up in a tree, where a limb has been
wrenched off by the wind or water has rotted a
hole (perhaps begun by a woodpecker) large
enough for their accommodation ; but now and
then a place is selected nearer the ground, as a
hollow log ; and Kennicott tells us that in the
open regions of Illinois and the neighboring States

it will occupy the burrows of other animals and even rear its progeny in them. It never digs a hole of any kind for itself; nor does it care for much bedding, — those in captivity preferring the bare boards of their pen to any litter that may be furnished to them. It is a forest animal, then, and rather inclined to swamps; but this may be merely because wet lands most often contain damaged trees, and also furnish more food than the hard, dry, upland groves. More rarely in the West, it takes excursions out on the prairies, doubtless in search of insects and crayfish.

In such a hole are produced in early spring a litter of five or six young ones that by and by grow large enough to leave home and follow the parents in their nocturnal vagabondage, staying with them for a year or so, until they found families of their own. Hence in the summer and autumn, when 'coons are mainly in evidence, they are most often met with in these little family companies. It is rare to see a wild 'coon out of doors in daylight, however; or, if he does appear, it is usually rolled up asleep in some lofty crotch, where he dozes in the sunshine, rocked by the breeze. In summer, however, when the young are old enough to travel, they move about a good deal, and in the West often leave the woods altogether and wander far out upon the prairies, taking shelter in the deserted holes of skunks, badgers, and similar temporary retreats. As winter comes

on they restrict their roving, seek a permanent
abode, and in the coldest weather hibernate completely.   This, however, is only in the North, and
even there they are liable to awake and stir around
during warm spells, and usually emerge from their
torpidity in February or early March.   They sleep
with their heads curled down against their stomachs and with their faces protected by the furry
wrap of the tail, so that they are mere balls of fur.
That they are often abroad in winter is manifest
from the mark in the snow of their feet, which
have five toes both before and behind.

These tracks show that, although the animal is
plantigrade, and when quiet stands on the whole
soles of his feet, like a bear, when he walks he
treads only on his toes.

The raccoon eats anything he can get hold of;
and Kennicott has summed up the matter so
tersely that I cannot do better than quote his
concise phrases.

"The raccoon," he says, "is omnivorous.   It eats
flesh of any kind, preying upon small birds and
mammals, when it can catch them, and sometimes
making destructive forays into the poultry-yard.
It devours birds' eggs whenever within reach, pro-
curing the eggs of woodpeckers by thrusting its
paws into their holes; it also watches turtles when
depositing their eggs in the sand, and, upon their
departure, digs them up.   This animal is fond of
fish, and displays remarkable dexterity in capturing

them with his fore paws. It is also a most successful frog-hunter, and may frequently be tracked
along the river's edge, where it has been searching
for frogs, crayfish, water-snails, and dead mussels.
In summer frogs often form a large portion of its
food, when some species leave the water and therefore are easily caught. Insects are eaten to some
extent, as are slugs and snails. It also feeds
largely upon various vegetables in summer; and
its particular fondness for green corn (maize) is
well known to every farmer. . . . In winter they
will occasionally eat the ripened grain, and have
been known to visit corn-cribs for that purpose.
They are also said to eat acorns, and to gnaw
through pumpkins to procure the seeds; probably,
like the bear, they feed more or less on berries.
In confinement they are exceedingly fond of sugar.
Like the squirrels and spermophiles, they sometimes dig up newly planted corn."

The common name along the southern coasts
of the United States for the small, narrow, tangled,
wild oysters that grow so abundantly in the salt-
marshes and inlets, is "'coon-oyster," in reference
to the practice of the raccoons, who come down
to feed upon them at high tide. It is an old tra-
dition, that the animals now and then get caught
by a big one closing upon its paw and holding it
until the tide rises and drowns the animal; but I
have never known of such a case, though I have
seen the animal searching the oyster-reefs in

broad daylight, as well as by the light of the harvest moon. I question whether it ever happens, for the 'coon is not only too quick-witted but too nimble to be caught in a trap acting so slowly as that.

He is as clever as a monkey with his front paws — and with the hind ones, too, for that matter. A palmist would find, curiously enough, the same arrangement of "lines" and "mounts" in his palm as in those of a cat or a weasel, and would deduce similarity of acumen and behavior to those animals and be more nearly right than palmists usually are. These palms seem to be extremely sensitive, and by them he is able to distinguish objects very nicely. The fore feet, in fact, are never still, but are everlastingly moving in examination of whatever is within reach; and to see one sit up with his back against a log, holding something to eat between his hind feet, and daintily picking away and handing morsels to his mouth with his paws, is irresistibly comic. An egg is thus managed without wasting a drop, the teeth breaking a small opening in one end, and the tongue lapping up the contents while the shell is held firmly in the feet.

Raccoons are fond of many kinds of fruit and berries. Dr. C. C. Abbot puts into his "Upland and Meadow" a pleasant note of experience on this point.

"There in a small gum-tree, largely overgrown by a fox-grapevine, sat a small raccoon . . . and simply stared without winking as I approached.

When within a dozen paces I saw that its chops were literally dripping with gore. There were no feathers at the foot of the tree or caught in the tangled undergrowth, and no bits of fur; but drops of blood were spattered everywhere. The poor thing must be wounded, I thought. Hoping, therefore, to put the creature out of its misery, I planned to reach it; but as I had no gun, I could only climb. This failed, but, as I was looking up the straight stem of the tree, the 'coon moved a little upward and outward, as though determined to keep the space between us unchanged. The ease of its movements did not suggest a wound or a weakness from loss of blood, and I was again at sea in the matter, but only for a moment. Scattered about the vine were single grapes and bunches of two and three. A beggarly show for grapes; but then their size made up for the lack of numbers. Each grape was black as anthracite, a perfect sphere an inch in diameter. Such grapes! No wonder the raccoon had jaws dripping with gore; no wonder the leaves below were spattered with purple blotches. Every grape was nigh to bursting with the richest of ruddy wild fruit-juices, crimson and blood-thick. My little 'coon was an epicure."

One of the singularities of the raccoon is its habit of dipping its food in water or washing it, to which it owes its specific name, — *lotor*, the washer. If water is not at hand, it will often rub it vigorously before eating it. Various explanations of this have been given ; but it is probable that the simplest — namely, that it seeks to wash the food — is the nearest the truth. An acquaintance of mine was once mischievous enough to give a captive 'coon a raisin covered with cayenne pepper, which kept the poor animal sneezing for half an hour. The next day he was given another ; but this time he sniffed at it in advance, and discovering more pepper, took the raisin to his dish and washed it. Smelling of it cautiously, he was not satisfied with his work, but continued to rub it between his palms and wash it under the water until he was sure nothing remained upon it to annoy his throat and nose.

The animal is partial to the water, being a good swimmer and loving to dwell near streams or the sea and to dabble in the shallows, fishing many a morsel out of the pools and capturing agile crabs and crayfish by overturning the stones.

His partiality for crayfish is notorious, those living in the far Southwest subsisting almost wholly upon these subterranean creatures, which they scratch out of their tubular burrows. This taste has given rise to a fable among the Ojibways, related by Dr. Henry Schoolcraft, long ago, in his "Algic Tales." The Indian story regards it as the result of an enmity between the two animals, in the fabulous antiquity, which caused such wariness on the part of the latter that the poor raccoon, with all his stealthiness, was at last put into great straits for a meal, since no crayfish would venture near shore. At length he bethought him of an expedient to decoy his enemy. Knowing that the crayfish feed on worms, he procured a quantity of old rotten wood (filled with worms), and stuffing it into his mouth and ears, and powdering it over his body, he lay down by the water's edge, to induce the belief that he was dead. An old crayfish came warily out of the water, and crawled around and over the body of his enemy; then called to his fellows:

"Assibun is dead, — come up and eat him!"

When a multitude had gathered the raccoon sprang up and devoured the whole crowd. While he was still busy with the fragments of his feast, a little female crayfish, carrying her infant sister on her back, came up, seeking her relatives. Discovering what had happened, she went boldly up to the monster, and said:

· "Here, Assibun, you behold me and my little sister. We are all alone. You have eaten up our parents and all our friends, — eat us, too."

Then she sang a long death-chant, the end of which was in this strain:

"Once my people, lodge and band,
  Stretched their numbers through the land;
  Roving brooks and limpid streams,
  By the moon's benignant beams.
  First in revel, dance, and play,
  Now, alas! ah! where are they?
  Clutch us, monster, — eat us soon
              Assibun, amoon."

The raccoon felt reproached by this act of courage and magnanimity, and refused to dishonor himself by exterminating the whole race.   At this moment Manabozha, the Deity, happened to pass by. Seeing how things were :

" Tyau !" he shouted to the raccoon. "Thou art a thief and an unmerciful dog. Get thee up into the trees, lest I change thee into one of these same wormfish, for thou wast thyself originally a shell, and bearest in thy name the influence of my transforming hand."

He then took up the little supplicant crayfish girls, and cast them into the stream.

" There," said he, " you may dwell. Hide yourself under the stones, and hereafter you shall be playthings for children."

Mr. Schoolcraft explains that the name of the raccoon, Assibun, in the Chippewa language, seems to be a derivation from the noun meaning *shell ;* but he says that no tale of a transformation, such as is here alluded to, has come to his knowledge. The raccoon also figures in another tale, where the giant (red-headed) woodpecker saves Manabozha from starving to death, on one occasion in winter, by digging out of a tree with his powerful bill a family of torpid 'coons, and laying them at the sovereign's feet.

Dr. Godman relates that a pair of raccoons in his keeping were never happy except when provided with a tub of water, in which they played incessantly; and never were gayer at this sport than in midwinter — this was in Philadelphia — paddling about and playing with fragments of floating ice. "Indeed," says Dr. Godman, "these animals have never evinced the slightest dislike to cold, or suffered in any degree therefrom; they have in all weathers slept in a flour-barrel thrown on its side, with one end entirely open, and without any material of which to make a bed. They show no repugnance to being sprinkled or dashed with water, and voluntarily remain exposed to the rain or snow, which wets them thoroughly, notwithstanding their long hair, which, being almost erect, is not well suited to turn the rain."

It is evident that creatures so tough as this would not waste much time in winter torpidity anywhere south of New York or St. Louis. Certainly they do not hibernate to any extent in southern New Jersey, where, by the way, they are becoming rare. Wherever hibernation does take place it is probably due more to hunger than to cold. Thus Mr. Burroughs tells us that in the western Catskills the 'coons appear in March and go "creeping about the fields, so reduced by starvation as to be quite helpless, and offering no resistance to my taking them up by the tail and carrying them home." It is at this inhospitable season that they come to the farmer's house, burrow under his haystacks in search of mice, and invade his poultry-yard; a little later, too, as soon as the frost is out of the ground, they capture more insects, noxious and otherwise, than at any other time, except, perhaps, when grasshoppers are prevalent. Some captive 'coons are 'cute about beguiling chickens within reach. Mr. C. L. Herrick relates, in his " Mammals of Minnesota," that his pet abstained for weeks from harming the hens and chickens until they lost all fear and clustered about the animal to pick up the crumbs whenever he was fed. Then suddenly he profited by this education and had many a good dinner off his dupes before his credit was lost. I have been told of another pet raccoon, in western Pennsylvania, which was kept chained in a yard and fed on bread and vegetables until he longed for flesh. One day he was observed to break up his bread between his palms and scatter the crumbs in a line from the uttermost reach of his tether to the mouth of his artificial burrow. Then he went and lay down, very quietly, as if asleep. The chickens wandering about struck the trail of crumbs, and innocently followed it up to the nose of the humbug in fur, who snatched one or more with a leap, and twisted their heads off. I cannot so vouch for the accuracy of observation here, as to be certain that the scattering of the crumbs was intentional; but I believe that such a device is quite within procyonine capability.

The prime delicacy of the world in the 'coon's opinion, however, is Indian corn, in that same

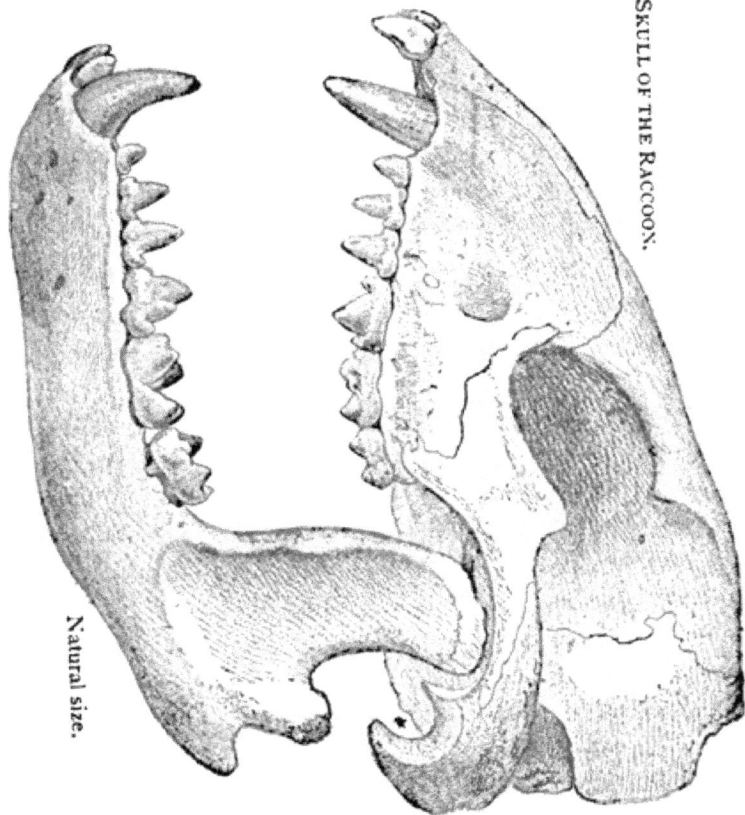

SKULL OF THE RACCOON.

Natural size.

287

milky condition of sweet half-ripeness which so
attracts the squirrels, the mice, the birds and —
you and me, if you please; and when he has
found it he strips back the husk as deftly as any
"neat-handed Phyllis," and disposes of the succulent kernels with ease and rapidity. This is his
occupation and delight in the still hot August
nights, and no one has pictured it forth to our imagination as delicately as does Rowland Robinson
in his "New England Fields and Woods":

"Above the katydid's strident cry and the
piper's [green cricket's] incessant notes, a wild,
tremulous whinny shivers through the gloom at
intervals, now from a distant field or wood, now
from the near orchard. One listener will tell you
that it is only a little screech-owl's voice, another
that it is the raccoon's rallying-cry to a raid on the
cornfield. There is endless disputation concerning
it, and apparently no certainty, but the raccoon is
wilder than the owl, and it is his voice that you hear.

"The corn is in the milk; the beast is ready.
The father and mother and well-grown children,
born and reared in the cavern of a ledge or hollow
tree of a swamp, are hungry for sweets remem-
bered or yet untasted, and they are gathering to
it, stealing out of the thick darkness of the woods
and along the brookside in single file, never stop-
ping to dig a fiery wake-robin bulb, nor to catch a
frog, nor to harry a late brood of ground-nesting
birds, but only to call some laggard, or distant

U

clansfolk. So one fancies, when the quavering cry is repeated and when it ceases, that all the freebooters have gained the cornfield and are silent with busy looting."

Now is the time when 'coon-hunting is most fun and best rewarded, for now the animal is so fat that a large one may weigh twenty-five pounds, and his flesh is tender, juicy, and well-flavored, whereas, at other times of the year, it is rather poor provender, even for a stew, and sometimes as rank as that of a muskrat; nevertheless, our colored friends in the South are willing to eat it at any time.

'Coon-hunting is one of the truly American sports of the chase, though its devotees have found difficulty in persuading folks to take their sport seriously. It is, in truth, a comical aspect of hunting, and is scarcely less wanting in dignity than a 'possum chase, which confessedly has none at all. If 'coon-hunting be regarded as a step higher than that, it loses the advantage at the end, for a fat 'possum is certainly better eating than a 'coon, however rotund. The chase, nevertheless, calls for endurance, since an old 'coon may run four or five miles after he has been started, zigzagging hither and yon, circling round and round trees, leaving a track calculated to make a dog dizzy, swimming streams, and running along the tops of logs and snake-fences, hiding his trail with the craftiness of a fox.

The hunt is always organized late at night.

Nobody ever heard of a real 'coon-hunt by daylight. The animals are moving about then, leaving trails that, starting at the edge of the woods,
lead into the fastnesses where they take refuge.
Such trails would grow "cold" before noonday.

There are dogs called 'coon-dogs, but of no
particular breed or pedigree. A local pack will
consist of Rag, Tag, and Bobtail, with all of Bobtail's friends and connections. One of them is
known to be best and takes the lead. They call
him the trailer. The rest rush yelping after, and
as fast as possible follow the hunters, with torches
or lanterns or by moonlight, carrying axes and
hatchets, guns, and antidotes for snake-bite in
flat, black bottles. Trailer's motley crew catch a
sniff of the trail and disappear in the darkness
of the brushy woods, baying, barking, yelping,
squealing, each after its kind. After them go the
whooping hunters, following by ear as the dogs do
by nose, for none can use the sense of sight. They
crash through the bushes, dodge the trees, but are
tripped up by the roots, stumble over logs and
rocks, bruise their legs against stumps and snags,
flounder into holes and puddles, are whipped by
elastic branches, scratched by briers, pierced by
thorns, drenched with dew, and spattered with mud
and dead leaves. The strongest get far ahead,
and calling on to the dogs and back to their fellows,
discourage instead of aid the breathless laggards
by their lessening voices.

Finally a chorus of eager barking in a different tone from what has thus far been heard announces to experienced ears that the dogs have some game at bay. The hunters dispute as to what it is as they crash and stagger on through the gloom, each swearing he knows by his cur's voice what sort of an animal he has in view. Arrived at the scene of the clamor, the dogs are found in frantic excitement around the foot of a tree, in whose shadowy foliage something is supposed to be hidden. Will it be a 'coon, or will it turn out a 'possum, a wild-cat, or mayhap an owl?

First of all a fire is lighted, and its upreaching blaze sends fitful rays of yellow light far among the overhanging branches. Now there may be discerned a hollow near the summit of the trunk, and as dead branches are heaped upon the fire sharp eyes may detect a triangular head peering out of what was once, perhaps, the front door of a woodpecker's home, and glints of green are reported to be the glare of a raccoon's eyes.

To shoot him there would now be easy enough, but the eager hunters have no wish to dispose of him so summarily. They have other uses to put him to. The Iroquois felt the same way when they had tracked and caught a Huron or a Jesuit. The nimblest man in the party is sent up the tree, and given a stick wherewith to frighten or poke or pry the cornered animal out of his castle. Compelled to leave the hole, it creeps out upon a limb,

and squatting down snarls at the stranger, who
tries to shake loose its hold. But this is a vain
attempt. A raccoon can cling like a burr. Try to
drag your pet 'coon off the top of a fence, and if
he chooses to resist, you may pull him limb from
limb before he will let go. So they take the severer
method of chopping the branches, until the poor
little beast has none left to clutch in falling, and
comes down a heap of fur and teeth and claws into
the midst of the dogs. Instantly there follows a
scrimmage, where often an honest bark is changed
in the middle to a yelp of pain, until many a time
the *mêlée* changes to a ring of hurt and angry but
vanquished curs around a 'coon lying on his back,
with bloody teeth and claws ready to try it again;
and then he is shot by the hunters, merciless to the
last. More often the whole tree must be cut down,
and the brave 'coon falls with it, and is dashed out
among his enemies to fight for his life at the end
of his fall. If meanwhile a large 'possum has been
taken alive, he is usually pitted against the 'coon,
and it is even betting which will win. This nocturnal foray, where the prey may be either an
opossum or a raccoon, or perhaps both, and now
and then a bear, is especially the sport of the
Southern negroes, who have got the name "coons"
in consequence, — that is, 'coon-hunters.

Young ones taken on these expeditions or in
traps — spring-traps are said to be most effective
when set under water, beside some lily-coated frog

pond — are often kept captive, and make interesting pets. They must be kept chained, however, or they will wander away and forget to return; and also because of their mischievous pranks. They grow slowly, and change from the summer to winter pelage by the loss of the under-fur in tufts, replaced by longer hair than forms the warm-weather coat. They are not only intelligent, but show marked love of companionship, a pair getting on together most lovingly, missing each other very decidedly when separated, and exhibiting some affection for their master. This, however, seems to depend, as it should, upon the animal's appreciation of kindness, for an abusive person will excite an undying enmity. Godman found that the common fear of their biting was not justified by their disposition, those he kept being entirely harmless even to little children; but they always instinctively bite when suddenly hurt, as might often happen from a careless child. He mentions that his young raccoons would spring in a fury and bite at the leg of a table or corner of a door against which they had knocked themselves in their play. Dr. Godman's account contains many other interesting and suggestive particulars as to their habits.

Another excellent history of pet raccoons is contained in Merriam's "Mammals of the Adirondacks," showing among other things their innate inquisitiveness and propensity for mischief, so that it will not do to give them the liberty a pet skunk enjoys.

"If not closely watched they will slyly enter the house through some open door or window, and are liable to do considerable damage, for their natural curiosity prompts them to examine everything within reach, and anything out of reach of a 'coon must be inaccessible indeed. They invariably manifest an insatiable desire to investigate the pantry shelves, and rarely neglect to taste every edible thing that happens to be there. They have a special *penchant* for sweetmeats, and greedily devour preserves, honey, molasses, sugar, pies, and cakes; and even bread, butter, lard, milk, etc., are by no means disregarded. They remove the covers from jars and pails, and uncork bottles, with as much ease and facility, apparently, as if they had been instructed in this art from earliest infancy. Doors that latch, as they do in most old country houses, are soon opened, even by unsophisticated 'coons, and it takes them but a short time to acquire the method of opening knob doors. Their fore paws are employed as hands, and can be put to almost as great a variety of uses as those of the monkey, — which animal they further resemble in the propensity for mischief-making."

The common raccoon is about thirty-three inches in length, of which from ten to eleven inches represent the tail; and when in good condition it will weigh about twenty pounds. The prevailing color is light gray, tinged with pale rusty across the shoulders and much overlaid with black-tipped hairs. The under parts are of a similar gray, without the black tips, and, like the rest of the body, allow the dull sooty brown under-fur to show through. The upper surfaces of the feet are whitish, the hind feet being about 4 inches in length, and the fore feet $2\frac{3}{4}$ inches. The brush of the tail is nearly uniform in diameter ($2\frac{1}{2}$ to 3 inches) throughout, only the end being rounded off. It has five distinct black rings, separated by grayish rusty intervals of about the same width, and the tip is black. The face shows a large oblique black patch on each cheek, continuous with paler ones beneath the jaws, and others behind the ears, which are whitish; this gives a spectacled appearance to the front face. The muzzle is naked and flexible. Specimens have been seen nearly black all over, and albinos are not infrequent.

The pelt of the raccoon is a valuable object when taken in cold weather, when the animal is in good condition. The fur is thick and warm, and the skin very durable. Hence it is in large demand in Canada and northern Europe for making coats, such as are worn by drivers and others that can afford something a little better than the sheepskin of the Russian peasant. North America furnishes half a million skins a year, nearly all of which are trapped in the region of the Great Lakes. The hair has been famous for felting purposes ever since the little beast became known to the pioneer fur-traders; and vast quantities of it are consumed in Germany and elsewhere to-day in the manufacture of hats. A 'coon-skin cap used to be the common headgear of the Western man of the early part of the century, and many of Washington's hardiest soldiers wore them with the ringed tail drooping behind as a barbaric ornament. The fur of the South American species is shorter and less dense.

Let us bid the 'coon farewell in the pleasant language of Rowland Robinson:

"This little brother of the bear is one of the few remaining links that connect us with the old times, when there were trees older than living men, when all the world had not entered for the race to gain the prize of wealth, or place, or renown; when it was the sum of all happiness for some of us to 'go a-'cooning.' It is pleasant to see the tracks of this midnight prowler, this despoiler of cornfields, imprinted in the mud of the lane or along the soft margin of the brook, to know that he survives, though he may not be the fittest. When he has gone forever, those who outlive him will know whether it was his quavering note that jarred the still air of the early fall evenings, or if it was only the voice of the owl — if he, too, shall not then have gone the inevitable way of all the wild world."

INDEX

299

BIRDCRAFT.

A FIELD-BOOK OF TWO HUNDRED SONG, GAME, AND WATER BIRDS.

By MRS. MABEL OSGOOD WRIGHT.

With Full-page Plates, containing 128 Birds in their Natural Colors, and Other Illustrations.

Small quarto. Cloth. $3.00.

PRESS COMMENTS.

"This is a charming volume, upon a pleasant theme. The author is not a hard-hearted scientist who goes forth with bag and gun to take life and rob nests, but a patient and intelligent observer, who loves the children of the air, and joins their fraternity. Such a book inspires study and observation, and encourages effort to acquire knowledge of the works of God. The book is a wise teacher as well as an inspiring guide, and contains beautiful, well-arranged illustrations." — *New York Observer.*

"The author has struck the golden mean in her treatment of the different birds, saying neither too much nor too little, but mostly furnishing information at first hand, or from approved authorities. The book will be very welcome to a large number who have felt the want of a work of this kind. It will increase their enjoyment of outward nature, and greatly add to the pleasure of a summer vacation." — *Boston Herald.*

THE FRIENDSHIP OF NATURE.

A NEW ENGLAND CHRONICLE OF BIRDS AND FLOWERS.

By MRS. MABEL OSGOOD WRIGHT.

18mo. Cloth. Gilt Top, 75 cts. ; Large Paper, $3.00.

Filled with the very spirit of New England woods and byways, it is a book to make glad the heart of every lover of nature; for, together with a keenness of insight, and a scientific precision, it unites the warmest sympathy and reverence of all the doings of that mysterious world of birds and flowers of which we really know so little and of which no study can be more engrossing. Mrs. Wright is well known as a photographer of unusual skill, and the large paper edition of her charming little book is illustrated by reproductions of her own pictures of the scenes she puts before us so vividly.

"A dainty little volume, exhaling the perfume and radiating the hues of both cultivated and wild flowers, echoing the songs of birds, and illustrated with exquisite pen pictures of bits of garden, field, and woodland scenery. The author is an intimate of nature. She relishes its beauties with the keenest delight, and describes them with a musical flow of language that carries us along from a 'May day' to a 'winter mood' in a thoroughly sustained effort; and as we drift with the current of her fancy and her tribute to nature, we gather much that is informatory, for she has made a close study of the habits of birds and the legendry of flowers." — *Richmond Dispatch.*

THE MACMILLAN COMPANY,
66 FIFTH AVENUE, NEW YORK.

TOMMY-ANNE

AND

THE THREE HEARTS.

BY

MRS. MABEL OSGOOD WRIGHT,

Author of "Birdcraft," "The Friendship of Nature," etc.

WITH MANY ILLUSTRATIONS BY

ALBERT D. BLASHFIELD.

12mo. Cloth. Colored Edges. $1.50.

This book was planned as a partial answer to the torrent of questions asked by a group of children living a wholesome out-door life — children who feel a kinship with living things, and have an inborn belief that there is something more in a flower, bird, or little wood beast than its market value ; children who are not satisfied with answers that give them the bare facts of nature with all the humanity squeezed out, but who on the other hand cannot be silenced with the pretty but impossible fables with which it was once considered proper to degrade the intelligence of youth.

" The ways of all wild living creatures have a fascinating interest for most children, but unfortunately their parents and friends are usually too ignorant to answer their reasonable questions. To such inquiring minds this book should be a boon.   They will hear the unappreciated garden Snake's plea for toleration, and Mole's account of his own good deeds. They will have a peep into Bob-o-link's wardrobe and a glimpse of Madam Duck's nursery, and will learn many surprising things about our small familiar beasts, and the common plants which we all think we know. A pleasant thread of story binds together the bits of information, making them easier to hold, and the child who reads will be charmed while he is instructed, and led on to make new discoveries himself."

— The Nation.

THE MACMILLAN COMPANY,

66 FIFTH AVENUE, NEW YORK.

BOOKS ON NATURE.

BADENOCH (L. N.). — **The Romance of the Insect World.** By L. N. BADENOCH. With Illustrations by MARGARET J. D. BADENOCH and Others. *Second Edition.* Gilt top. $1.25.

"The volume is fascinating from beginning to end, and there are many hints to be found in the wisdom and thrift shown by the smallest animal creatures." — *Boston Times.*

"A splendid book to be put in the hands of any youth who may need an incentive to interest in out-door life or the history of things around him." — *Chicago Times.*

BRIGHTWEN. — **Inmates of My House and Garden.** By Mrs. BRIGHTWEN. Illustrated. 12mo. $1.25.

"One of the most charming books of the season, both as to form and substance." — *The Outlook.*

"The book fills a delightful place not occupied by any other book that we have ever seen." — *Boston Home Journal.*

GAYE. — **The World's Great Farm.** Some Account of Nature's Crops and how they are Grown. By SELINA GAYE. With a Preface by G. S. BOULGER, F.L.S., and numerous Illustrations. 12mo. $1.50.

The University of California expressly commends this to its affiliated secondary schools for supplementary reading.

"It is a thoroughly well-written and well-illustrated book, divested as much as possible of technicalities, and is admirably adapted to giving young people, for whom it was prepared, a readable account of plants and how they live and grow." — *Public Opinion.*

"One of the most delightful semi-scientific books, which every one enjoys reading and at once wishes to own. Such works present science in the most fascinating and enticing way, and from a cursory glance at paragraphs the reader is insensibly led on to chapters and thence to a thorough reading from cover to cover. . . . The work is especially well adapted for school purposes in connection with the study of elementary natural science, to which modern authorities are united in giving an early and important place in the school curriculum." — *The Journal of Education.*

THE MACMILLAN COMPANY,

66 FIFTH AVENUE, NEW YORK.

HUTCHINSON. — **The Story of the Hills.** A Book about Mountains for General Readers and Supplementary Reading in Schools. By H. N. HUTCHINSON, author of "The Autobiography of the Earth," etc. Illustrated. $1.50.

"A book that has long been needed, one that gives a clear account of the geological formation of mountains, and their various methods of origin, in language so clear and untechnical that it will not confuse even the most unscientific." — *Boston Evening Transcript.*

"It is as interesting as a story, and full of the most instructive information, which is given in a style that every one can comprehend. . . ."
— *Journal of Education.*

INGERSOLL. — **Wild Neighbors.** A Book about Animals. By ERNEST INGERSOLL. Illustrated. 12mo, Cloth. $1.50.

JAPP (A. H.). — **Hours in My Garden,** and Other Nature-Sketches. With 138 Illustrations. $1.75.

"It is not a book to be described, but to be read in the spirit in which it is written — carefully and lovingly." — *Mail and Express.*

"It is a book to be read and enjoyed by both young and old."
— *Public Opinion.*

POTTS (W.). — **From a New England Hillside.** Notes from Underledge. By WILLIAM POTTS. *Macmillan's Miniature Series.* 18mo, 75 cents.

"But the attraction of Mr. Potts' book is not merely in its record of the natural year. He has been building a house, and we have the humors and the satisfactions, and hopes deferred, that usually attend that business. He has been digging a well, and the truth which he has found at the bottom of that he has duly set forth. . . . Then, too, his village is Farmington, Conn., and there Miss Porter has her famous schoo's, and her young ladies flit across his page and lend their brightness to the scene. And, moreover, he sometimes comes back to the city, and he writes pleasantly of his New York club, the Century. Last, but not least, there are lucubrations on a great many personal and social topics, in which the touch is light and graceful and the philosophy is sound and sweet." — *Brooklyn Standard-Union.*

WEED. — **Life Histories of American Insects.** By Professor CLARENCE M. WEED, New Hampshire College of Agriculture and Mechanical Arts. Fully Illustrated. Cloth. $1.50.

THE MACMILLAN COMPANY,
66 FIFTH AVENUE, NEW YORK.

4